Marinades

Also by Melanie Barnard
365 More Ways to Cook Chicken
Low-Fat Grilling
The Best Covered and Kettle Grills Cookbook Ever
With Brooke Dojny
Parties!
Cheap Eats

Marinades

The Secret of Great Grilling

MELANIE BARNARD

HarperPerennial
A Division of HarperCollins*Publishers*

HarperCollins books may be purchased for educational, business, or sales promotional use. For information please write: Special Markets Department, HarperCollins Publishers, Inc., 10 East 53rd Street, New York, NY 10022.

FIRST EDITION

Designed by Nancy Singer

Library of Congress Cataloging-in-Publication Data

Barnard, Melanie.
    Marinades : the secret of great grilling / Melanie Barnard.
       p. cm.
    Includes index.
    ISBN 0–06–095162–1
    1. Marinades. 2. Barbecue cookery. I. Title.
TX819.M26B37   1997
641.8'14—dc20   96-26200

---

99 00 01 ❖/RRD 10 9

*This book is dedicated to Bob Cornfield,
without whom I would never
have become a published grilling guru.*

Contents

Acknowledgments

Grilling is more fun as a group activity. So is writing a book. Like the food from my backyard grill, a cookbook becomes delicious only when many people inspire, taste, test, and ask for seconds. My thanks go first to my family, especially my husband, who co-chairs the grilling guru position in our neighborhood, and my gurus-in-training sons, who have carried the message (and a couple of my grills) off to their own homes. I will always be grateful for the friendship of my cooking and writer compatriot, Brooke Dojny, for she is the fuel upon which I have always stoked my writing fire. And I am further blessed to have my editor and friend Susan Friedland, whose belief in a grilling book "trilogy" has made this effort possible.

Introduction

After thirty years of grilling all manner of foods, in every kind of weather, and with practically any equipment that supports a fire, I've concluded that great grilling depends mostly on marinades, sauces, and rubs. Though a great grill, a sunny day, and a nice piece of swordfish are a good beginning, the real secrets of great grilling lie in those little things that gild the grilled lily—subtle marinades with a fresh herb infusion, wildly spiced and peppery rubs, or signature lip-smacking sauces are what leave lingering memories of great grilling.

Every neighborhood has one grilling guru. It's that person whose backyard smells so good that it turns heads and noses and practically stops traffic from blocks away. It's the guy who sends

1

out inviting smoke signals every Saturday and Sunday, and usually midweek, too. And it's the woman who always has people leaning over the fence, and whose kids are especially popular around suppertime.

It doesn't much matter if the guru has a fancy 6-burner gas grill or a fold-up aluminum beach cooker. Expensive wood chips are nice, but they don't appear to have any impact on the griller's local fame. Nor does it seem to be the kind of food that makes the difference. Any backyard griller will be glad to tell you about the grill or the chips or where he bought the steak, but notice that the grilling guru rarely gives away the real secret—the sauce/marinade/rub.

It is with much pride that I attest to being the grilling guru in my neighborhood, and having already written two books on the subject has further solidified my position.

Unlike some other grilling gurus, however, I am happy to share my secrets with you. In fact, it would be my great honor if you would use them as inspiration in your own efforts to becoming the grilling guru of your neighborhood.

HOW TO USE THIS BOOK

The recipes in this book are versatile. Each marinade, sauce, rub, or condiment complements more than one type of food. In order to make them most accessible for you, I've given measurement yields for every recipe, along with a range of suggested uses, such as burgers, chicken breasts, fish steaks, vegetables, etc. After choosing your meat/poultry/seafood/vegetable/fruit, you can refer to the master chart that follows for recommended <u>total</u> cooking times. Even if you are a novice, you will find that very soon you won't need to refer to the chart and will come to rely on your own instincts about grilling times and temperatures. All of the recipes in the book work well in both gas and charcoal grills. Those that utilize medium heat are also well suited to electric grills.

CUT OF MEAT	WEIGHT OR SIZE	GRILL TEMPERATURE	DIRECT OR INDIRECT	TIME	TEST FOR DONENESS	NOTES
BEEF						
Sirloin or round steak	1 inch thick;	hot	direct	13 to 18 minutes total for medium-rare	pink in center	cut across the grain to serve
Flank Steak	½- to ¾-inch thick	hot	direct	8 to 16 minutes total	pink in center	cut across the grain to serve
Filet Mignon Steak	1 inch thick (about 5 ounces)	hot	direct	6 to 8 minutes total	pink in center	
Whole Tenderloin	5 pounds	medium-hot	indirect	25 to 30 minutes total	pink in center	
Skirt Steak	¼- to ½-inch thick	hot	direct	4 to 6 minutes total	barely pink in center	slice across the grain to serve
Kebabs	1½-inch chunks	hot	direct	6 to 8 minutes total	pink in center	
Ribs	cut crosswise into 2-inch chunks	hot	direct	grill or bake marinated meat wrapped in heavy-duty foil for 1 to 1½ hours, then unwrap and grill 8 to 10 minutes total	very tender with richly browned exterior	

CUT OF MEAT	WEIGHT OR SIZE	GRILL TEMPERATURE	DIRECT OR INDIRECT	TIME	TEST FOR DONENESS	NOTES
BEEF *(continued)*						
Burgers	¾ inch thick (5 to 6 ounces each)	medium-hot	direct	10 to 12 minutes	no trace of pink in center	
PORK						
Center-Cut Chops	¾ inch thick (about 6 ounces each)	medium-hot	direct	15 to 18 minutes	no trace of pink remaining	
Boneless Chops	½ to ¾ inch thick (about 4 ounces each)	medium-hot	direct;	10 to 14 minutes	no trace of pink remaining	
Shoulder Steaks	½ inch thick	medium	direct	25 to 30 minutes	no trace of pink remaining	brush with marinade or seasoned water during grilling to keep moist
Tenderloin Roast	about 1 pound	medium-hot	direct	15 to 20 minutes	no trace of pink remaining	

Spareribs	3 pounds	medium-hot	direct or indirect	1½ hours	well-browned crisp exterior, tender interior with no trace of pink remaining	if cooking over direct heat, first precook wrapped in heavy-duty foil for 1 hour, then place directly on grill for 30 minutes. If using indirect, cook on grill for 1½ hours
Fully Cooked Ham Half	4 to 4 ½ pounds	medium	indirect	1 hour	internal temperature should be 140 degrees	
Ham Steak	¾ to 1 inch thick	hot	direct	8 to 10 minutes	browned on the outside and heated through	
Raw Link Sausages	1 link	medium-hot	direct	8 to 10 minutes	no trace of pink remaining	precook first by simmering in water or wine until nearly cooked through, about 10 minutes

CUT OF MEAT	WEIGHT OR SIZE	GRILL TEMPERATURE	DIRECT OR INDIRECT	TIME	TEST FOR DONENESS	NOTES
PORK (*continued*)						
Cooked or Smoked Sausages or Frankfurters	4-inch link or piece	hot	direct	5 to 10 minutes	browned	
LAMB						
Loin or Rib Chops	1 inch thick	medium-hot	direct	9 to 12 minutes	barely pink in center	
Steaks or Shoulder Chops	½ inch thick	medium-hot	direct	5 to 7 minutes	barely pink in center	
Boned and Butterflied Leg	3 pounds	medium-hot	direct	20 to 25 minutes	barely pink in center	
Kebabs	1½-inch cubes	hot		6 to 8 minutes total	barely pink in center	
VEAL						
Loin Chop	1 inch thick (about 8 ounces)	medium-hot	direct	15 to 17 minutes	white throughout	
CHICKEN						
Whole Broiler-Fryer	3 pounds	medium	indirect	1¼ to 1½ hours	juices run clear	

	Weight/Size	Heat	Method	Time	Doneness
Half	1¼ to 1½ pounds	medium-hot	indirect	1 hour	juices run clear
Breast Halves	6 to 8 ounces each	medium-hot	direct	22 to 27 minutes total	white throughout
Thighs and Drumsticks	4 to 8 ounces each	medium-hot	direct	27 to 33 minutes	juices run clear
Boneless Skinless Breasts	4 to 5 ounces each	medium-hot	direct	12 to 16 minutes	white throughout
Breast Cutlets	2 to 3 ounces each	hot	direct	3 to 6 minutes	white throughout
Boneless Skinless Thighs	4 ounces each	medium-hot	direct	14 to 17 minutes	no longer pink
White or Dark Meat Kebabs	1½-inch chunks	medium-hot	direct	11 to 14 minutes	juices run clear
TURKEY					
Whole Breast	6 to 8 pounds	medium	indirect	1 to 1½ hours;	internal temperature of 170 degrees; white throughout
Drumstick	½ to 1 pound	medium	indirect	50 to 60 minutes	internal temperature of 170 degrees; juices run clear

CUT OF MEAT	WEIGHT OR SIZE	GRILL TEMPERATURE	DIRECT OR INDIRECT	TIME	TEST FOR DONENESS	NOTES
TURKEY (continued)						
Breast Tenderloin Steak	4 to 6 ounces	medium-hot	direct	11 to 14 minutes	white throughout	
Breast Cutlets	3 to 4 ounces each	medium-hot	direct	5 to 7 minutes	white throughout	
SEAFOOD						
Steaks	¾ to 1 inch thick	medium-hot	direct	7 to 10 minutes	opaque throughout	
Fillets	½ to ¾ inch thick	medium-hot	direct	5 to 8 minutes	opaque throughout	
Kebabs	1- to 1½-inch chunks	medium-hot	direct	6 to 9 minutes		
Shrimp	large or jumbo	medium-hot	direct	4 to 6 minutes	opaque throughout	large shrimp best done on a skewer to avoid falling through grates, but jumbo can be done on grill rack; can be grilled peeled or unpeeled

Scallops	large sea	medium	direct	3 to 5 minutes	opaque throughout	
Clams	hard-shell	medium	indirect	5 to 8 minutes	shells are open	discard any clams that do not open
Lobster	1½ pounds, cut in half	medium	indirect	12 to 14 minutes	opaque throughout	lobsters can be split live or parboiled for 3 minutes in boiling salted water, then split and grilled
VEGETABLES						
Asparagus	thick stalks	medium	direct	9 to 11 minutes		
Belgian Endive	whole head	medium	direct	6 to 9 minutes		
Broccoli	large florets	medium	direct	6 to 9 minutes		parboil in boiling salted water for 2 minutes and drain

CUT OF MEAT	WEIGHT OR SIZE	GRILL TEMPERATURE	DIRECT OR INDIRECT	TIME	TEST FOR DONENESS	NOTES
VEGETABLES (*continued*)						
Corn	1 ear	medium	direct or indirect	15 to 25 minutes		if grilling in the husk, soak first in water for 30 minutes. Shucked corn takes less time
Eggplant	½- to ¾-inch slices	medium	direct	10 to 15 minutes		
Fennel	1 bulb; quartered	medium	direct	5 to 8 minutes		
Leeks	1 medium; trimmed	medium	direct	5 to 7 minutes		
Peppers; any color bell	whole or quartered	medium	direct	8 to 14 minutes	skins blackened and flesh tender	
Potatoes	small whole red or 1½-inch chunks	medium	direct	7 to 9 minutes	precook in boiling salted water until nearly tender, about 8 minutes	

Squash, Summer	sliced lengthwise about ¼ inch thick	medium	direct	4 to 8 minutes	
Squash, Winter	halved or quartered	medium	direct	10 to 15 minutes	precook in microwave or oven until nearly tender, 30 minutes to 1 hour, depending upon type of squash
Sweet Potato	sliced lengthwise ¼ inch thick	medium	direct	7 to 9 minutes	
Tofu; extra-firm	sliced about ½ inch thick	medium-hot	direct	6 to 10 minutes	blot off any excess moisture before grilling, turn carefully one time during grilling until golden on the outside
Tomatoes; meaty	sliced ½ inch thick	medium	direct	4 to 6 minutes	turn carefully one time during grilling

GRILLING BASICS

Grilling is the oldest and simplest form of cookery, and is an integral part of the world's great cuisines. As backyard grillers, we have a fine cooking lineage, and we are also in good company considering that top chefs and restaurants often grill food to add taste and style. Though grilling is easy to do, it is well worth the time to learn a few basics if you are a novice.

Know Your Grill

It is far less important whether you have a gas or charcoal grill than it is to understand your unit, and that means reading the instruction manual before stoking up your first fire.

Charcoal grills vary widely in their configurations and price ranges. Be sure to buy a covered grill, and not an open brazier. The cover gives you much more flexibility and temperature control, as well as the ability to grill in all sorts of weather conditions. The smoke and fire are controlled by both the level of the grill rack and the position of the upper and lower air vents. Follow the manufacturer's directions, then make adjustments for your own taste and the idiosyncrasies of your particular grill. Always be aware that a charcoal grill contains an open fire—never leave it unattended, keep children and pets at a distance, and remember that the coals will still be burning for several hours after you finish cooking.

Each *gas grill* manufacturer touts a slightly different configuration and style of heat elements—at the lowest end is a single-burner portable grill fired by a butane canister, and at the upper level are permanent installations of 3- or 4-burner outdoor cookstoves attached to underground gas lines. No matter what type of gas grill you have, the safety instructions for ignition should always be followed, and the gas turned off at the source after use. Some models even allow for the addition of wood chips, or have metal spits for cooking roasts, or sport side burners for warming sauces and boiling water for corn on the cob.

Electric grills are getting better every year, but they still do not heat to the temperatures needed to sear meats, poultry, and seafood properly. They are fine for most uses, and ideal if your building or neighborhood codes prohibit charcoal or gas grilling. Preheat them according to the manufacturer's directions and treat them with the same safety standards you apply to your electric kitchen stove-top burners.

Home Smokers are increasingly popular because the newer models are both easy and fun to use, and produce really fine results. The best are the offset types in which the covered firebox can be used for direct grilling, while at the same time producing smoke that wafts into a larger box holding the food to be smoked. This indirect heat configuration gives far better temperature control than the torpedo-shaped units in which the firebox is in the bottom with the food stacked on top.

BUILDING THE FIRE

Gas and electric grills are simple—just turn them on. Building a charcoal fire is a bit more trouble, but made much easier these days with the availability of several reliable fire starters.

Some upper-end grills come with a butane or propane *gas-fired igniter*, which some feel combines the best of the gas and charcoal grilling worlds.

My favorite of the less expensive starters, most of which work on all grills, is the *electric starter coil*, which is nothing more than a loop-shaped electric element. When placed in the center of a pyramid of charcoal, it ignites the charcoal. Be sure to cool the element on a heatproof surface away from children and pets. The coil's major limitation is that you must be near a source of electricity.

Also fairly infallible is the *chimney starter*, which is a simple perforated metal canister in which charcoal is placed in the top and newspaper is stuffed into the bottom. The unit is set in the firebox, then the newspaper is ignited with a match. In about 20 minutes, the coals in the top will be glowing, and are then used as "seeds" to ignite other coals in the firebox.

Chemical liquids and solid block starters are reliable, but be sure to allow at least 30 minutes for the chemicals to burn off before cooking. Never add chemicals to a lit fire.

Kindling is, of course, the original fire starter, and still works just fine, though this is probably the most difficult way. Start with a bed of loosely rolled newspaper, then place dry twigs over the newspaper. Make a small pyramid of charcoal over the twigs, then ignite the newspaper. In about 20 minutes, the coals should be ignited.

FUELING THE FIRE

Pure hardwood charcoal is my first choice for fueling a charcoal grill or smoker. It burns hotter and longer than briquettes, and can sometimes even be reused along with the addition of some new coals. It can be a bit more expensive and harder to find, but is well worth seeking out.

Good quality *charcoal briquettes*, which are more readily available, also work very well, and I prefer the kinds with the least amount of chemicals. Be sure to build your charcoal fire at least 30 minutes before cooking so that the coals will be evenly ignited and burn down to the proper cooking temperature.

For thousands of years before auto magnate Henry Ford invented charcoal briquettes, *hardwood* was the fuel of choice for grilling. It still makes the most aromatic fire, although a pure hardwood fire is tricky to ignite and to control. A good compromise is to use charcoal and add hardwood chunks or chips for aroma.

ENHANCING THE FIRE

All of the marinades, sauces, rubs, and pastes in this book are designed to enhance the food to be grilled, but it doesn't hurt to gild the lily occasionally.

Aromatic wood chips or chunks add a definite character to the

ɩɩɩ   MARINADES

fire and food cooked over it. Hickory is certainly the most assertive, and is best used on foods that can stand up to it, such as beef and pork. Mesquite has a characteristic woodsy flavor that gives a subtly sophisticated aroma to beef, lamb, vegetables, and fish steaks. Fruit woods, such as maple, cherry, or peach give a pleasant flavor to poultry, fish, and pork, and are especially nice if fruit is to be grilled as part of the recipe. All wood chips should be soaked in water for at least 20 minutes and added to the fire shortly before cooking.

Grapevine cuttings and sturdy *herb branches* such as rosemary, can be tossed onto the fire just before cooking or near the end of cooking time to give a boost to delicate items such as seafood and vegetables. Select herbs that reflect the recipe ingredients. Fresh grapevine cuttings and herb branches do not need to be soaked before they are added to the fire.

THE RIGHT TEMPERATURE

Outdoor grilling is at best an imprecise and variable method of cooking. Air temperature, wind conditions, and type of fuel all contribute to the temperature of the coals in the grill. Fortunately, grilling is also very forgiving. If you pay attention to your grill, you won't go very far wrong. Your eyes and your nose are your best guides to doneness. But to help you along, here is a hand test to roughly determine the grill temperature. The optimum temperatures for the recipes in this book are given in the same terminology.

Hot fire: The coals glow red, and you can hold your hand 6 inches from the fire for no more than 3 seconds.

Medium-hot fire: The coals are gray but with a red underglow, and you can hold your hand 6 inches above the coals for no more than 5 seconds.

Medium fire: The coals are gray with only a hint of red, and you can hold your hand 6 inches above the fire for no more than 7 seconds.

Grill Safety

All grills are open fires, and should be treated with respect. Important things to remember include:

~ Position the grill in an open area well away from the house, dry leaves, or combustibles.

~ Never leave a grill unattended. Wind, dogs, and children can easily knock it over.

~ Never add starter fluid after the fire is ignited.

~ Keep a fire extinguisher, bucket of sand, or pail of water nearby in case of an emergency.

~ Remember that the coals will continue to burn for several hours after cooking, and a smoker may have hot coals for up to 48 hours.

~ Turn off the gas and unplug the electricity at the source when you are finished cooking on a gas or electric grill.

~ Do not wear loose, flowing clothing near an open flame.

Marinades

〜 〜 〜 〜 〜 〜 〜 〜 〜

Marinades

The word "marinade" is derived from the Latin or Italian "marinara," meaning of the sea. Like seawater, the original marinades of many centuries ago were briny solutions meant to preserve, tenderize, and flavor foods. Though today we have other ways to keep meats (like refrigerators), marinating remains one of the most popular ways to add interest and character to foods, especially those that are to be grilled.

The basic components of a liquid marinade are acid, such as vinegar, citrus juice, tomatoes, or wine, and seasonings, such as whole or ground spices and fresh or dried herbs. The acid acts to break down the surface tissue of the food placed in it while the seasonings add flavor. Sometimes the acid can be a bit harsh, and salty seasonings can draw moisture out of the food. In these cases, a small amount of oil is usually part of the marinade, as the oil acts as a protector to the food and restores some of the moisture as well. In general, the leaner the food, the more likely it is to need oil in the marinade.

Because all marinades contain an acid, it is important to use nonreactive containers for marinating. Aluminum and other metals may discolor upon prolonged contact with acid and may even have a chemical reaction that may cause an unpleasant taste. Glass or ceramic dishes or heavy-duty zipper-style food storage bags can be used.

Unless there is a lot of marinade, it is better to use a shallow dish so that more of the food will be covered by the liquid. If it is not totally covered, be sure to turn the food in the marinade at least once per hour. The plastic bag works especially well since it can simply be turned over and over.

Marinating times vary widely depending upon the food. Delicate foods such as fish, shellfish, and boneless chicken breasts should be marinated for the least amount of time—seafood should not marinate more than an hour, and boneless chicken breasts only up to about 2 hours. After that, the tissues will break down so much that the cooked food will be beyond tender and become mushy in texture. Veal and lean pork cuts such as tenderloin roast or boneless chops also require relatively short marinating times, usually less than 4 hours. Beef is more sturdy, and the tougher cuts such as flank steak or brisket can marinate for 24 hours or more without loss of texture quality. Marinating at room temperature is quicker, but any food to be marinated for longer than 1 hour should be placed in the refrigerator.

Marinades do not penetrate more than about ½ inch into the food, so the most flavor is imparted to thinner cuts. Longer marinating times will not give deeper penetration, but instead will simply impart a stronger marinade taste to the outer portion of the food.

Do not use leftover marinade as a barbecue sauce or condiment unless it has been boiled for at least 5 minutes to destroy any harmful bacteria that may have been transferred to the marinade from the raw food. If you know you will be using the marinade as a sauce, make extra in the beginning and reserve a portion separately. Do not reuse a marinade. All marinades are easy to prepare, and it isn't worth risking the danger of bacterial contamination to the newly marinated food.

SPANISH BAROLO
AND CAPER MARINADE

ζ ζ ζ ζ ζ ζ ζ ζ ζ

Makes about 1⅓ cups; enough to marinate
2 to 3 pounds of beef, lamb, or venison, 3 duck breasts
or dark meat chicken, drumsticks or thighs

If you don't have any Barolo wine, use another spicy red wine.
Small capers have more flavor than the giant ones. Use a zester to
easily make thin strips of citrus zest that will adhere to and
caramelize on the meat during grilling.

¾ cup Barolo wine
⅓ cup sherry wine vinegar
2 tablespoons extra-virgin olive oil
3 tablespoons drained small capers
2 teaspoons dried marjoram
2 teaspoons finely julienned orange zest
2 garlic cloves, minced

In a small bowl, whisk together all ingredients. Place meat or
fowl in a shallow glass or ceramic dish in a single layer. Add marinade, turning food to coat. Cover and refrigerate, turning occasionally, 2 hours for fowl, and 6 to 12 hours for meat.

WASABI MUSTARD MARINADE

*Makes about 1⅓ cups; enough to marinate
1½ pounds of tuna or swordfish steak
or sirloin steak cut ¾ to 1 inch thick*

Wasabi powder is a dehydrated Japanese horseradish that, when reconstituted, is usually used as a condiment. Here, it gives a real kick to tuna or swordfish or thin cuts of beefsteak.

*1½ tablespoons wasabi powder
1 tablespoon dry mustard
⅓ cup sake or dry sherry
⅓ cup reduced-sodium soy sauce
⅓ cup rice wine vinegar
1½ tablespoons grated fresh ginger*

In a small bowl, stir the wasabi powder and dry mustard into the sherry until dissolved. Stir in the remaining ingredients. Place fish or meat in a single layer in a glass or ceramic dish. Add marinade, turning food to coat. Cover and refrigerate, turning occasionally, about 1 hour for fish and 2 hours for meat.

CHIMMICHURRI MARINADE

≀ ≀ ≀ ≀ ≀ ≀ ≀ ≀ ≀

Makes about 1 cup; enough to marinate
1 to 1½ pounds of beefsteak or lamb chops
cut about 1 inch thick

This is a classic seasoning mix in Argentina, where beef is king. Sherry wine vinegar has a rich depth that needs very little oil to offset the acid. Flat-leaf parsley, when really fresh from the garden or the market, has a wonderful, peppery flavor. Lavishly garnish the finished steaks with more parsley.

½ cup sherry wine vinegar
2 tablespoons extra-virgin olive oil
⅓ cup chopped flat-leaf parsley, plus 2 tablespoons for garnish
2 teaspoons dried oregano
6 large garlic cloves, minced
¾ teaspoon dried hot red pepper flakes

In a small bowl, combine all ingredients. Place meat in a single layer in a glass or ceramic dish. Add marinade, turning food to coat. Cover and refrigerate, turning occasionally, 1 to 3 hours for lamb chops and 2 to 4 hours for beefsteak.

TOASTED SESAME MARINADE

ι ι ι ι ι ι ι ι ι

*Makes about 1⅓ cups; enough to marinate
1½ pounds of beefsteak, 2 ½ pounds of pork chops,
or 4 pounds of baby back pork ribs*

Toasted sesame seeds have an entirely different and far richer flavor than untoasted. Toasted sesame oil is similarly complex. If you use this for pork ribs, they don't really need any other sauce during grilling.

¼ *cup sesame seeds*
⅔ *cup rice wine vinegar*
½ *cup reduced-sodium soy sauce*
¼ *cup packed dark brown sugar*
2 tablespoons toasted sesame oil
1 teaspoon dried hot red pepper flakes

In a small skillet, toss the sesame seeds over medium heat just until the color deepens to gold and the seeds become fragrant, about 2 minutes. Immediately remove from the skillet to prevent burning. Let cool. In a small bowl, combine the toasted seeds and the remaining ingredients. Place meat in a single layer in a glass or ceramic dish. Add marinade, turning food to coat. Cover and refrigerate, turning occasionally, 1 to 3 hours for beefsteak or pork chops, and 2 to 4 hours for ribs.

Thai Red Curry Marinade

~ ~ ~ ~ ~ ~ ~ ~ ~

Makes about 1⅓ cups; enough to marinate
2 ½ pounds of bone-in chicken or pork chops
or 2 pounds of pork tenderloin

All kinds of prepared curry pastes are readily available now, including red, green, mussaman, and pantang. They are made by a variety of companies that specialize in Thai ingredients, and are packaged in small jars or plastic pouches. Ingredients vary by manufacturer, so read the labels and avoid those made with modified starches as their flavor is less intense. The red curry called for here is among the hottest of all, but it is tempered by the coconut milk in the marinade.

1 cup unsweetened coconut milk, regular or low-fat
¼ cup red curry paste
¼ cup fresh lime juice
3 tablespoons chopped cilantro
1½ tablespoons vegetable oil

In a small saucepan, heat the milk and curry paste over low heat, stirring for about two minutes just until the paste dissolves. Pour the mixture into a small bowl and let cool slightly. Stir in the lime juice, cilantro, and oil. Place chicken or meat in a single layer in a glass or ceramic dish. Add marinade, turning to coat. Cover and refrigerate, turning occasionally, 1 to 3 hours for chicken or pork chops or pork tenderloin.

KOREAN BEEF RIB MARINADE

Makes about 1⅓ cups; enough to marinate about 4 pounds of beef ribs or 2 pounds of chuck roast

Beef ribs are not often used in this country, but in Korea, they are a popular barbecue dish. If you use really good quality back ribs, they can be cooked entirely on the grill. Short ribs are best when given a head start of about 1 hour in a covered pan in a 350-degree oven or wrapped in foil before grilling. A boneless chuck roast can be cooked in the same way.

½ cup cider vinegar
½ cup reduced-sodium soy sauce
⅓ cup orange juice
2 tablespoons dark molasses
¼ cup chopped fresh ginger
2 tablespoons paprika
1 tablespoon grated orange zest
4 large garlic cloves, minced
½ teaspoon coarsely ground black pepper

In a small bowl, whisk together the vinegar, soy sauce, orange juice, and molasses. Whisk in remaining ingredients. Place meat in a single layer in a glass or ceramic dish. Add marinade, turning to coat. Cover and refrigerate, turning occasionally, 6 to 12 hours.

MOROCCAN SPICED LEMON MARINADE

ₑ ₑ ₑ ₑ ₑ ₑ ₑ ₑ ₑ

Makes about ¾ cup; enough to marinate 2 split
game hens, 2 pounds of bone-in chicken,
or 1 pound of swordfish or tuna or shark steaks

Halved game hens seem just right for this lusty marinade. Loosen the skin so that the flavors can permeate the meat during marinating. Since fish takes very little marinating time, let the marinade stand for about 30 minutes first so that the dried herbs will soften and release their oils into the marinade.

½ cup fresh lemon juice
3 tablespoons extra-virgin olive oil
4 garlic cloves, minced
1 tablespoon grated lemon zest
2 teaspoons coarsely ground black pepper
2 teaspoons dried thyme
2 teaspoons dried oregano
2 teaspoons dried rosemary
1 teaspoon ground cardamom
1 teaspoon ground cumin
½ teaspoon salt

In a small bowl, whisk together all ingredients. Place poultry or seafood in a single layer in a glass or ceramic dish. Add marinade, turning to coat. Cover and refrigerate, turning occasionally, 1 to 3 hours for poultry or 1 hour for fish.

BAGNA CAUDA
MARINADE

ا ا ا ا ا ا ا ا ا

Makes about 1 cup; enough to marinate 1½ pounds
of skinless, boneless chicken breasts or thighs,
tuna or swordfish steaks, or jumbo peeled
and deveined shrimp

Bagna cauda means "warm bath" and is a classic Italian dipping
sauce for raw vegetables. It is also a heady bath for boneless
chicken breasts or tuna or swordfish steaks. Don't leave out the
anchovies—they make all the difference!

6 tablespoons fresh lemon juice
3 tablespoons extra-virgin olive oil
1 can (2 ounces) flat anchovies
¼ cup chopped scallions
6 garlic cloves, minced
2 teaspoons grated lemon zest
¾ teaspoon coarsely ground black pepper

In a small bowl, whisk together the lemon juice and oil. Add
the anchovies, mashing with the back of a spoon. Stir in the scallions, garlic, lemon zest, and pepper. Place chicken or seafood in a
single layer in a glass or ceramic dish. Add marinade, turning to
coat. Cover and refrigerate, turning occasionally, 1 to 2 hours for
chicken, and 30 minutes to 1 hour for seafood.

Asian Ginger Lime Marinade

ι ι ι ι ι ι ι ι ι

*Makes about 1 cup; enough to marinate 1½ pounds
of skinless, boneless chicken breasts or thighs,
jumbo peeled and deveined shrimp or sea scallops, or
fish fillets such as grouper or snapper*

Fresh ginger is crisp and juicy with a very sharp, spicy flavor. If
your ginger is soft and very stringy, its potency is greatly dimin-
ished. Buy a new "knob," grate what you need, and freeze any
extra. Use the medium holes in the grater—fine holes will produce
ginger juice. Nam pla, hoisin sauce, and hot chile sauce are all
available at Asian markets, but most large supermarkets also carry
them in the Chinese food section.

6 tablespoons fresh lime juice
3 tablespoons nam pla (Thai fish sauce)
3 tablespoons hoisin sauce
3 tablespoons hot chile sauce
3 tablespoons grated fresh ginger

In a small bowl, combine all ingredients. Place chicken or
seafood in a single layer in a shallow glass or ceramic dish. Add
marinade, turning or stirring to coat. Cover and refrigerate, turning occasionally, 1 to 2 hours for chicken, 30 minutes to 1 hour
for fish, and 30 minutes for shellfish.

DELICATE THAI HERB
AND SPICE MARINADE

ı ı ı ı ı ı ı ı ı

Makes about 1 cup; enough to marinate 1½ pounds
of jumbo peeled and deveined shrimp or large sea
scallops or 1 pound of boneless pork chops
or pork tenderloin

Fresh herbs and spices give this marinade a distinctly summery
feeling, especially well suited to shellfish. A bed of mixed cilantro,
mint, and basil is a sophisticated plate presentation. Sprinkle the
top of the grilled seafood with chopped peanuts.

½ cup unsweetened coconut milk, regular or low-fat
¼ cup fresh lemon juice
2 tablespoons peanut oil
3 tablespoons finely chopped fresh lemongrass or 1 tablespoon
*   grated lemon zest*
2 tablespoons chopped fresh basil
2 tablespoons chopped fresh cilantro
2 tablespoons chopped fresh mint
1 tablespoon grated fresh ginger
2 garlic cloves, minced
1 jalapeño pepper, seeded and minced
3 tablespoons chopped peanuts

In a small bowl, whisk together the coconut milk, lemon juice,
and oil. Stir in remaining ingredients. Place seafood or pork in a
shallow glass or ceramic dish. Add marinade, turning to coat.
Cover and refrigerate, turning occasionally, 30 minutes for seafood,
1 to 2 hours for pork chops, and 2 hours for pork tenderloin.

MONTEGO BAY CURRIED COCONUT MARINADE

ι ι ι ι ι ι ι ι ι

*Makes about 1½ cups; enough to marinate
3 pounds of bone-in chicken, 3 halved game hens,
or 2 pounds of pork chops*

This is an adaptation of a marinade recipe given to me by a Jamaican cooking friend. She uses English bitter orange marmalade, but sweet orange marmalade works just as well if you increase the lime juice to about ⅓ cup. Unsweetened coconut is available in health food stores. It toasts nicely on the grill, so be sure to pat it into the poultry or meat after marinating. The amount of hot pepper sauce depends on the heat of the brand. Start with the lesser amount and increase it next time.

⅔ cup unsweetened coconut milk, regular or low-fat
¼ cup bitter orange marmalade
¼ cup fresh lime juice
2 teaspoons Worcestershire sauce
1 or 2 teaspoons liquid hot pepper sauce to taste
¼ cup grated unsweetened coconut
3 garlic cloves, minced
1 Scotch bonnet or jalapeño pepper, seeded and minced

In a small saucepan, heat the coconut milk with the marmalade over medium-low heat, stirring just until marmalade melts, about 2 minutes. Pour into a small bowl and let cool slightly. Stir in the remaining ingredients. Place chicken or pork in a single layer in a glass or ceramic dish. Add marinade, turning to coat. Cover and refrigerate, turning occasionally, 2 to 3 hours.

POLYNESIAN PASSION FRUIT AND RUM MARINADE

ﾐ ﾐ ﾐ ﾐ ﾐ ﾐ ﾐ ﾐ ﾐ

*Makes about 1 cup; enough to marinate 1 pound
of skinless, boneless chicken breasts or thighs,
firm fish fillets such as grouper or snapper, fish steaks
such as shark or swordfish or salmon, or shellfish
such as large peeled and deveined shrimp*

Passion fruit juice or nectar is available in health food stores. Guava or apricot nectar are other options in this lively, fresh-tasting marinade.

*⅔ cup passion fruit juice or nectar
2 tablespoons fresh lemon juice
2 tablespoons fresh lime juice
2 tablespoons dark rum
3 tablespoons chopped cilantro
1 teaspoon grated lemon zest
1 teaspoon grated lime zest
½ teaspoon dried hot red pepper flakes
¼ teaspoon salt*

In a small bowl, whisk together the juices and rum. Stir in the cilantro, lemon and lime zests, pepper flakes, and salt. Place chicken, fish, or shellfish in overlapping layers in a glass or ceramic dish. Add marinade, turning or stirring to coat. Cover and refrigerate, turning occasionally, 1 to 2 hours for chicken, 30 minutes to 1 hour for fish, and 30 minutes for shellfish.

INDONESIAN SATAYS

ꙅ ꙅ ꙅ ꙅ ꙅ ꙅ ꙅ ꙅ ꙅ

Makes about 1⅓ cups; enough to marinate
1½ pounds of skinless, boneless chicken breasts or
thighs, beef or pork tenderloin, or tuna or shark steaks

Satays are Indonesian appetizers grilled on bamboo sticks—the
Southeast Asian equivalent of the Middle Eastern shish kebab. There
are as many variations of these pork, beef, chicken, or seafood tidbits
as there are cooks who make them, but many have dipping sauces
based on peanuts and chiles. This marinade reflects those tastes and
the result is so flavorful that no extra sauce may be needed at all.

½ *cup rice wine vinegar*
⅓ *cup chunky or creamy peanut butter*
¼ *cup fresh lime juice*
3 tablespoons reduced-sodium soy sauce
2 tablespoons unsulphured molasses
¼ *cup chopped cilantro*
1 tablespoon grated fresh ginger
3 large garlic cloves, minced
1 teaspoon grated lime zest
½ *teaspoon dried hot pepper flakes*

In a small bowl, whisk together the vinegar and peanut butter
until well blended. Stir in the remaining ingredients. Cut chicken,
meat, or fish into 1-inch chunks and place in a glass or ceramic
dish. Add marinade, stirring to coat. Cover and refrigerate, stirring
occasionally, about 1 hour for chicken or meat, and about 30 minutes for fish.

THREE-ONION AND WORCESTERSHIRE MARINADE

ζ ζ ζ ζ ζ ζ ζ ζ ζ

Makes about 2 cups; enough to marinate
3 pounds of flank or sirloin steak or brisket

This is especially good on flank steak or brisket. For a really tender brisket, place meat and marinade in a baking dish. Cover and bake for about 1½ hours before finishing directly on the grill for about 1 hour more. Accentuate the flavors by grilling some sweet onion slices along with the steak or brisket. If you can get fresh imported bay leaves, try them here. Otherwise, use a good quality of dried bay leaves. Check for freshness by breaking a leaf in half—it should break nicely into two pieces, not into dry shreds.

1 cup good-quality beer
¼ cup malt vinegar
¼ cup Worcestershire sauce
2 tablespoons stone-ground mustard
1 onion, chopped
4 scallions, chopped
2 garlic cloves, minced
2 bay leaves, broken in half

In a medium bowl, whisk together the beer, vinegar, Worcestershire sauce, and mustard. Stir in the onion, scallions, garlic, and bay leaves. Place meat in a glass or ceramic dish. Add marinade, turning to coat. Cover and refrigerate 8 to 24 hours.

SHANGHAI GARLIC
FIVE-SPICE MARINADE

ﻉ ﻉ ﻉ ﻉ ﻉ ﻉ ﻉ ﻉ ﻉ

*Makes about 1½ cups; enough to marinate 5 pounds
of pork spareribs, 3 pounds of boneless leg of lamb,
2 ½ pounds of duck breasts, or 2 split game hens*

Chinese five-spice powder is a commercial blend of fennel, anise, licorice root, cinnamon, and cloves. Its sweet and tangy taste plays well against the sharpness of grated ginger and hot red pepper flakes for a simple marinade with a very complex taste. Its assertiveness is especially good with pork ribs, boneless leg of lamb, duck breasts, or game hens.

⅔ cup reduced-sodium soy sauce
⅓ cup rice wine vinegar
3 tablespoons oyster sauce
1 tablespoon vegetable oil
2 teaspoons hot chili oil
2 tablespoons grated fresh ginger
1 tablespoon Chinese five-spice powder
½ teaspoon hot red pepper flakes
4 garlic cloves, minced

In a small bowl, combine all ingredients. Place the meat or poultry in a single layer in a glass or ceramic dish. Add the marinade, turning to coat. Cover and refrigerate, turning occasionally, 6 to 12 hours for meat, and 2 to 4 hours for poultry.

ADOBO MARINADE

~ ~ ~ ~ ~ ~ ~ ~ ~

Makes about 1¼ cups; enough to marinate
1½ pounds of skinless, boneless chicken, boneless
pork chops, or firm fish such as snapper,
grouper, or mahimahi

Adobo is probably the most common marinade in the Cuban kitchen. The primary ingredients are garlic, cumin, oregano, and sour orange or lime juice, although every cook adds his or her own personal touch. Mexican adobos usually contain orange juice and smoked chiles, while Puerto Rican mixes have a high vinegar content. No doubt, the original adobos, like all marinades, were meant to preserve and tenderize, but today flavoring is the most important reason.

5 garlic cloves
¾ teaspoon salt
2 teaspoons dried oregano
½ teaspoon ground cumin
½ teaspoon dried thyme
⅓ cup red wine vinegar
⅓ cup fresh orange juice
⅓ cup fresh lime juice
2 tablespoons vegetable oil
¼ cup chopped flat-leaf parsley

(continued)

Mash the garlic with the salt to make a paste. Scrape into a small bowl and stir in the oregano, cumin, and thyme. Whisk in the remaining ingredients. Place chicken, meat, or fish in a shallow glass or ceramic dish. Add marinade, turning to coat. Cover and refrigerate 1 to 2 hours for chicken or meat, and 30 minutes to 1 hour for fish.

PROVENÇAL RASPBERRY AND SHALLOT MARINADE

ₗ ₗ ₗ ₗ ₗ ₗ ₗ ₗ ₗ

*Makes about 1⅓ cups; enough to marinate 2 pounds
of skinless, boneless chicken breasts, large or jumbo
peeled and deveined shrimp, large sea scallops,
or fish such as monkfish or halibut*

As simple and delicate as a summer morning in Provence, this marinade is ideal for chicken breasts, fish, and shellfish. Commercial herbes de Provence is a blend of dried rosemary, marjoram, thyme, sage, anise seed, and savory. For the most flavor, be sure your jar is not more than a few months old.

½ cup dry white wine
½ cup raspberry or other fruit vinegar
⅓ cup chopped shallots
1 tablespoon herbes de Provence
½ teaspoon salt
½ teaspoon coarsely ground black pepper

In a small bowl, combine all ingredients. Place chicken or seafood in a shallow glass or ceramic dish. Add marinade, turning or stirring to coat. Cover and refrigerate, turning occasionally, 1 to 2 hours for chicken and 30 minutes to 1 hour for seafood.

TARRAGON MUSTARD MARINADE

Makes about 1¼ cups; enough to marinate 1½ pounds
of skinless, boneless chicken breasts or thighs,
2 split game hens, 1½ pounds of jumbo
or large peeled and deveined shrimp, or sea scallops,
or 1½ pounds of firm fish such as monkfish or halibut

Tarragon-flavored vinegar is enhanced by chopped fresh tarragon and fortified with dry vermouth in this subtly assertive marinade that works well for all sorts of poultry and seafood.

½ cup dry vermouth
⅓ cup tarragon-flavored vinegar
1½ tablespoons Dijon mustard
1 tablespoon extra-virgin olive oil
2 tablespoons chopped fresh tarragon
½ teaspoon coarsely ground black pepper

In a small bowl, whisk together the vermouth, vinegar, mustard, and oil. Stir in the tarragon and pepper. Place the chicken or seafood in a shallow glass or ceramic dish. Add the marinade, turning or stirring to coat. Cover and refrigerate, turning occasionally, 1 to 2 hours for chicken and 30 minutes to 1 hour for seafood.

AVERY ISLAND
TABASCO COUNTRY
MARINADE

ι ι ι ι ι ι ι ι ι

*Makes about 1¼ cups; enough to marinate 1½ pounds
of beefsteak or pork tenderloin, 2 pounds bone-
in chicken thighs or drumsticks, or 1½ pounds
turkey steaks*

The McIlhenny family has been manufacturing Tabasco sauce on Avery Island, in Louisiana, for over 125 years. A museum on the island traces the history of the searingly hot red sauce, as well as that of its recent cousin, a milder green sauce. You may use either one here, but I remain partial to the original hot sauce.

*½ cup dry white wine
¼ cup white wine vinegar
2 tablespoons red or green Tabasco or other hot pepper sauce
1 tablespoon vegetable oil
1 tablespoon honey
1 teaspoon dried thyme
½ teaspoon ground cumin
¼ cup chopped scallions
2 garlic cloves, minced*

In a small bowl, whisk together the wine, vinegar, Tabasco sauce, oil, honey, thyme, and cumin. Stir in the scallions and garlic. Place meat or poultry in a shallow glass or ceramic dish. Add the marinade, turning to coat. Cover and refrigerate, turning occasionally, 2 to 4 hours for beef or pork, and 1 to 2 hours for poultry.

MARSEILLES FISHERMAN'S MARINADE

ɹ ɹ ɹ ɹ ɹ ɹ ɹ ɹ ɹ

Makes about 1¼ cups; enough to marinate 1½ pounds
of tuna or swordfish steaks or monkfish fillets,
1½ pounds of jumbo or large peeled and deveined shrimp,
or 2 ½ pounds bone-in chicken thighs or drumsticks

Taking its inspiration from the savory seasonings in bouillabaisse, that classic Mediterranean seafood stew, this marinade is meant for fish and shellfish, but is also good with duck and dark meat of chicken

¾ cup red wine
¼ cup red wine vinegar
2 tablespoons extra-virgin olive oil
1 tablespoon Pernod or other anise liqueur
3 garlic cloves, minced
2 tablespoons chopped fresh rosemary or 2 teaspoons dried
2 tablespoons chopped fresh thyme or 2 teaspoons dried
2 tablespoons chopped fresh summer savory or 2 teaspoons dried
2 tablespoons chopped fresh marjoram or 2 teaspoons dried

In a small bowl, whisk together all ingredients. Place fish, shellfish, or chicken in a shallow glass or ceramic dish. Add the marinade, turning or stirring to coat. Cover and refrigerate, turning occasionally, 30 minutes to 1 hour for fish or shellfish, or about 2 hours for chicken.

MINTED GRAPEFRUIT
AND HONEY MARINADE

ι ι ι ι ι ι ι ι ι ι

*Makes about 1¼ cups; enough to marinate
1½ pounds of skinless, boneless chicken breasts
or turkey breast cutlets*

Grapefruit is good for much more than breakfast! Here, it is the
basis for a pleasantly tangy Floridian marinade for chicken or
turkey. If you make this in winter, at the height of grapefruit season, you may broil instead of grill without loss of flavor.

1 cup fresh grapefruit juice
3 tablespoons vodka
1 tablespoon honey
3 tablespoons chopped fresh mint
1 tablespoon grated grapefruit zest
2 teaspoons grated fresh ginger
1 teaspoon ground coriander seed
1 jalapeño pepper, seeded and minced

In a small bowl, whisk together the grapefruit juice, vodka,
and honey. Stir in remaining ingredients. Place the poultry in a
shallow glass or ceramic dish. Add the marinade, turning to coat.
Cover and refrigerate, turning occasionally, 1 to 2 hours.

BELLINI MARINADE

*Makes about 1¼ cups; enough to marinate 1½ pounds
skinless, boneless chicken breasts, turkey cutlets,
or fish such as monkfish or mahimahi, and more than
enough to macerate 4 peeled and halved peaches*

The famous Venetian cocktail is the inspiration for this light and summery marinade for delicate fish and chicken. It is also quite nice for fruit to be grilled, including peaches, of course.

½ cup peach nectar
½ cup champagne vinegar
2 tablespoons fresh lemon juice
2 tablespoons crème de cassis
1 tablespoon grated lemon zest
1 tablespoon extra-virgin olive oil
½ teaspoon coarsely ground black pepper
¼ teaspoon salt

In a small bowl, combine all ingredients. Place the poultry, fish, or fruit in a shallow glass or ceramic dish, and add marinade, turning to coat. Cover and refrigerate, turning occasionally, 1 to 2 hours for poultry, 30 minutes to 1 hour for fish, and about 10 minutes for fruit.

CAROLINA MOUNTAIN MARINADE

*Makes about 1¼ cups; enough for 2 pounds of
pork loin or 3 pounds of pork chops. Double recipe
for a 4-pound pork shoulder*

The sweet, hot, and sour characteristics of this marinade are typical of the pork barbecues in the Carolinas. If you don't want to do a whole pork shoulder, boneless pork will do quite nicely and take far less time. The same mixture can be used as a moppin' sauce for pork chops.

1 cup cider vinegar
2 tablespoons dark brown sugar
2 tablespoons liquid hot pepper sauce
2 tablespoons vegetable oil
1 teaspoon dried hot pepper flakes

In a small saucepan, heat the vinegar and brown sugar, stirring just until sugar dissolves. Remove from heat and stir in remaining ingredients. Let cool. Place pork loin or chops in a shallow glass or ceramic dish, and place pork shoulder in a deep mixing bowl. Add marinade, turning to coat. Cover and refrigerate, turning occasionally, 2 hours for pork loin, 1 hour for pork chops, and 12 to 24 hours for pork shoulder.

TRIPLE CITRUS AND PICKLED PEPPER MARINADE

ʒ ʒ ʒ ʒ ʒ ʒ ʒ ʒ ʒ

Makes about 1⅓ cups; enough to marinate
1½ pounds of skinless, boneless chicken breasts
or thighs, pork chops, or jumbo peeled
and deveined shrimp

Orange, lime, and lemon juices team up with heady spices for a real Caribbean flavor. Pickled peppers add heat, but not as much as in a jerk marinade, making this a good start for those just beginning to delve into the wonderful world of hot and spicy foods.

⅔ *cup orange juice*
¼ *cup fresh lime juice*
¼ *cup fresh lemon juice*
1 *tablespoon vegetable oil*
2 *to 3 tablespoons chopped pickled jalapeño peppers*
1 *tablespoon grated orange zest*
2 *teaspoons grated lime zest*
2 *teaspoons grated lemon zest*
6 *whole cloves*
6 *whole allspice*
2 *bay leaves, broken in half*
1 *cinnamon stick, broken in half*
½ *teaspoon ground mace*
½ *teaspoon salt*
½ *teaspoon coarsely ground black pepper*

(continued)

In a small dish, whisk together the citrus juices and oil. Stir in the remaining ingredients. Place the chicken, pork, or seafood in a shallow glass or ceramic dish. Add the marinade, turning to coat. Cover and refrigerate, turning food occasionally, 1 to 2 hours for chicken or pork, and 30 minutes for shrimp.

TANDOORI MARINADE

Makes about 1½ cups; enough to marinate 2 pounds
of skinless, boneless chicken or pork
and/or vegetable kebabs.

The tandoor is an ancient oven, with its origins in the Middle East. The primitive insulated oven is the forerunner of our very popular brick and clay ovens, but an updated version of the tandoor is still very much in use in India where tender flat breads are baked directly on the walls and floor of the oven, and meats and poultry are roasted to moist doneness on spits or skewers. Aromatic dry rubs, pastes, and marinades are a part of tandoor cooking, and this fragrant mix is inspired by the classic seasonings as well as the turmeric that lends the characteristic golden color.

1 cup plain low-fat yogurt
2 tablespoons fresh lemon juice
1 small onion, chopped
3 tablespoons finely chopped fresh ginger
4 garlic cloves, minced
1 teaspoon ground cumin
1 teaspoon ground turmeric
¾ teaspoon ground coriander
¾ teaspoon ground allspice
¾ teaspoon ground cinnamon

¾ teaspoon salt
½ teaspoon cayenne
⅛ teaspoon ground cloves

In a small bowl, stir together all of the ingredients. Cut bone-less chicken or pork into 1½- to 2-inch chunks, and cut vegetables into similar size pieces or thick slices. Place the chicken, pork, or vegetables in a shallow glass or ceramic dish. Add the marinade, stirring to coat. Cover and refrigerate, stirring food occasionally, 1 to 2 hours for chicken or pork, or 10 minutes for vegetables.

ANISE AND BALSAMIC MARINADE

ı ı ı ı ı ı ı ı ı

Makes about 1 cup; enough to marinate 1 pound
of skinless, boneless chicken breasts or thighs,
boneless veal, jumbo or large peeled and deveined shrimp,
or firm fish such as swordfish or monkfish

Toasting deepens and enriches the flavors of seeds and nuts. Here, a second toasting occurs during grilling, resulting in a really mem-orable marinade. Of course, the adjunct additions of balsamic vinegar, orange juice, and anise liqueur further enhance and com-plement the toasted anise seed making a marinade almost good enough for sipping!

2 tablespoons anise seed
½ cup balsamic vinegar
2 tablespoons extra-virgin olive oil
2 tablespoons frozen orange juice concentrate, thawed
2 tablespoons anisette or other anise liqueur
½ teaspoon salt
½ teaspoon coarsely ground pepper

(continued)

Toast the anise seeds in a small skillet over medium heat, tossing and stirring almost constantly until they become fragrant and are a shade darker, about 2 minutes. Immediately transfer seeds to a small bowl. Add the remaining ingredients to the bowl.

Place the chicken, meat, or seafood in a shallow glass or ceramic dish. Add the marinade, stirring or turning to coat. Cover and refrigerate, stirring occasionally, 1 to 2 hours for chicken or veal, and 30 minutes to 1 hour for seafood.

DILLED BUTTERMILK MARINADE

ı ı ı ı ı ı ı ı ı

Makes about 1⅓ cups; enough to marinate 2 ½ pounds
of veal chops cut about 1 inch thick
or 1½ pounds of salmon steaks or fillets

Buttermilk, like yogurt, is a fabulous marinade base. The enzymes act as natural tenderizers, and the thickness coats and protects delicate cuts of meat and seafood. With dill and red onion, it is ideal for salmon steaks and fillets or veal chops.

1 cup low-fat buttermilk
½ cup chopped red onion
¼ cup snipped fresh dill
1 tablespoon grated lemon zest
½ teaspoon cayenne
2 garlic cloves, minced

In a small bowl, combine all ingredients. Place veal or fish in a shallow glass or ceramic dish. Add the marinade, turning to coat. Cover and refrigerate, stirring occasionally, about 2 hours for veal and about 1 hour for fish.

MAPLE, SAGE, AND CIDER MARINADE

ι ι ι ι ι ι ι ι ι ι

Makes about 1½ cups; enough to marinate
1 small turkey breast or 2 pork tenderloins,
about ¾ pounds each

Somehow these three ingredients conjure up autumnal culinary images, such as roasting pork or turkey. Both of these can be done nicely on a grill, especially with pork tenderloins and turkey breast. If you wish, soak apple or acorn squash slices for a few minutes in the marinade, then grill alongside the meat or poultry.

1 cup apple cider
½ cup maple syrup
½ cup cider vinegar
3 tablespoons chopped fresh sage or 1 tablespoon crumbled dried
½ teaspoon salt
½ teaspoon coarsely ground pepper

In a small saucepan, gently boil the cider for 5 to 7 minutes until it is reduced to ½ cup. Let the cider cool, then combine it with the remaining ingredients in a small bowl. Place the turkey or pork in a shallow glass or ceramic dish. Add the marinade and turn to coat. Cover and refrigerate, turning occasionally, 2 to 4 hours for turkey and about 2 hours for pork.

ALEHOUSE STEAK
MARINADE

*Makes about 2 cups; enough to marinate
2 to 2 ½ pounds of beef*

Lean but naturally tough "commoner" flank, chuck, and round steaks turn into tender, juicy "kings" of the steak world after spending time in this pub-inspired marinade.

1 cup ale or beer
½ cup reduced-sodium beef broth
½ cup spicy tomato juice, such as V-8
2 teaspoons Worcestershire sauce
½ teaspoon hot pepper sauce, such as Tabasco
2 bay leaves, broken in half
1 teaspoon dried oregano
1 teaspoon dried thyme

In a small bowl, combine all ingredients. Place the meat in a shallow glass or ceramic dish. Add the marinade, turning to coat. Cover and refrigerate, turning occasionally, 4 to 24 hours.

SUMMER SAUERBRATEN MARINADE

ι ι ι ι ι ι ι ι ι

Makes about 1½ cups; enough to marinate
1½ pounds of beef round, flank or chuck steak,
or boneless chuck roasts

The classic German marinade for beef pot roasts translates well to grilled beefsteak and small roasts, too.

1 cup dry red wine
½ cup cider vinegar
1 onion, sliced
8 whole allspice
8 whole cloves
2 teaspoons whole black peppercorns
4 juniper berries or 2 tablespoons gin
2 thin slices fresh ginger

In a small bowl, combine all ingredients. Place meat in a shallow glass or ceramic dish. Add marinade, turning to coat. Cover and refrigerate, turning occasionally, 6 to 24 hours.

TANGERINE TAMARI
MARINADE

ʾ ʾ ʾ ʾ ʾ ʾ ʾ ʾ ʾ

Makes about 1½ cups; enough to marinate
1½ pounds of boneless, skinless chicken breasts
or thighs or duck breasts, 2 pounds of pork chops,
1½ pounds of jumbo or large peeled and
deveined shrimp, or shark or tuna steaks

When fresh tangerines are out of season, use frozen tangerine juice and grated orange zest instead. Taking cues from Pacific Rim and Caribbean cuisines, this marinade is my version of grilling ecumenism. Its rich and varied background makes it a good mix with a wide variety of meats, fowl, and seafood—politically and tastefully correct for any event!

½ cup rice wine vinegar
½ cup tangerine juice
2 tablespoons fresh lime juice
2 tablespoons toasted sesame oil
1 tablespoon Chinese-style prepared mustard
¼ cup chopped fresh cilantro
1 tablespoon grated tangerine or orange zest
¾ teaspoon ground cumin
¼ to ½ teaspoon hot red pepper flakes

In a small bowl, whisk together the vinegar, juices, oil, and mustard. Stir in the remaining ingredients. Place the poultry, meat, or seafood in a shallow glass or ceramic dish. Add the marinade, turning or stirring to coat. Cover and refrigerate, turning occasionally, 1 to 2 hours for chicken or duck, 1 to 3 hours for pork, and 30 minutes to 1 hour for seafood.

WINGS MARINADE

Makes about ¾ cup;
enough to marinate 1 to 1½ pounds
of chicken wings or drumsticks

A little bit of this marinade goes a long way. Rather than a soak, it is more of a coating and should be rubbed into all the nooks and crannies of chicken wings. It also makes a terrific coating for drumsticks, turning the famous Buffalo bar snack into a supper main course. The heat will vary considerably depending upon the brand of hot pepper sauce that you use.

3 tablespoons fresh lemon juice
2 tablespoons cider vinegar
2 tablespoons vegetable oil
2 tablespoons Worcestershire sauce
2 tablespoons liquid hot pepper sauce
1 tablespoon honey

In a small bowl, combine all ingredients. Place chicken in a shallow glass or ceramic dish. Add the marinade, turning to coat. Cover and refrigerate, turning occasionally, 1 to 3 hours.

JAMAICAN JERK MARINADE

≀ ≀ ≀ ≀ ≀ ≀ ≀ ≀ ≀

*Makes about 1¼ cups; enough
to marinate 2 to 2 ½ pounds of bone-
in chicken, pork chops, or cabrito (goat)*

Scotch bonnet chiles are about the size of jalapeños, but some think they are even hotter. The difference is a matter of degrees, all of which are searing. But Scotch bonnets are the chiles of choice in a jerk marinade. If you can only get jalapeños, no one will know the difference!

*¼ cup white wine vinegar
¼ cup fresh lime juice
2 tablespoons vegetable oil
1 tablespoon molasses
¼ cup chopped scallions
1 to 2 tablespoons minced Scotch bonnet or jalapeño chiles
1 cinnamon stick, broken in half
6 whole cloves
6 whole allspice
6 whole black peppercorns
½ teaspoon salt*

In a small bowl, whisk together the vinegar, lime juice, oil, and molasses. Stir in remaining ingredients. Place chicken, pork, or *cabrito* in a shallow glass or ceramic dish. Add the marinade, turning to coat. Cover and refrigerate 1 to 3 hours for chicken, 2 to 4 hours for pork, and 2 to 6 hours for *cabrito*.

HUNGARIAN PAPRIKA YOGURT MARINADE

~ ~ ~ ~ ~ ~ ~ ~ ~

Makes about 1½ cups; enough
to marinate 2 ½ pounds of pork
or veal chops or 2 pork tenderloins

Hungarian paprika is well worth the price—it has far more character than common supermarket paprikas. Like other spices, paprika loses potency over time, so don't buy more than you will use in a few months. Store the containers in a cool, dark, dry place such as a cupboard and not on a decorative spice rack in the center of the kitchen.

1 cup plain low-fat yogurt
3 tablespoons fresh lemon juice
1 small onion, chopped
3 tablespoons Hungarian or other high-quality paprika
3 garlic cloves, minced

In a small bowl, stir together all ingredients. Place the meat in a shallow glass or ceramic dish. Add the marinade, turning to coat. Cover and refrigerate 2 to 4 hours.

WINTER MINT MARINADE

Makes about 1¼ cups; enough to marinate
2 ½ to 3 pounds of boneless leg of lamb,
2 pounds of beefsteak, or 1 small turkey
or medium turkey breast

Just because your garden mint is covered with snow doesn't mean that your grill is also buried. For those of us who are in the Polar Bear Grilling Club (which includes anyone who grills outside regularly while wearing gloves and boots), this is a great minty marinade for lamb or beef or even a turkey. Don't try it on Thanksgiving, however. There is a limit as to how far your family will let you go with this grilling thing. I know. I tried it. Once.

½ cup dry white wine
¼ cup white wine vinegar
¼ cup bottled mint sauce
3 tablespoons mint jelly
2 large garlic cloves, minced
2 teaspoons dried mint

In a small saucepan, heat together the wine, vinegar, mint sauce, and jelly over low heat just until the jelly is melted. Stir in the garlic. If you are using the marinade for skin-on turkey, loosen the skin with your fingers and rub the dried mint onto the flesh under the skin. For lamb or beef, add the mint to the marinade. Place the meat in a shallow glass or ceramic dish. Place the turkey in a large heavy-duty plastic bag. Add the marinade to the dish or bag. Cover the dish or close the bag and place it in a pan. Refrigerate, turning occasionally 2 to 6 hours for lamb, 2 to 3 hours for beef, and 2 to 6 hours for poultry.

SHERRIED SHIITAKE
MARINADE

ʔ ʔ ʔ ʔ ʔ ʔ ʔ ʔ ʔ

Makes about 1 cup;
enough to marinate 1 to 1½ pounds
of thin steaks, such as skirt steaks,
or boneless pork chops

Dried mushrooms make an excellent flavoring agent. Here, dried shiitakes are reconstituted in a small amount of liquid, then pureed with other flavorings to form the marinade base. Other dried mushrooms can be used depending upon availability and preference.

½ cup dry sherry
½ ounce dried shiitake or other dried mushrooms
¼ cup reduced-sodium soy sauce
¼ cup red wine vinegar
2 tablespoons finely chopped shallots
1 tablespoon chopped fresh tarragon or 1 teaspoon dried
1 large garlic clove, minced
¼ teaspoon coarsely ground pepper

In a small saucepan, heat the sherry just to a simmer over medium heat. Put the mushrooms in a small bowl and pour the sherry over the mushrooms. Let the mushrooms stand for about 15 minutes until soft. Remove the mushrooms and strain the soaking liquid to remove all sediments. Puree the mushrooms with the strained soaking liquid in a food processor, then add the remaining ingredients and process a few seconds just until mixed. Place the meat in a shallow glass or ceramic dish. Add the marinade, turning to coat. Cover and refrigerate, turning occasionally, about 1 hour.

SAKE TERIYAKI MARINADE

Makes about 1¼ cups;
enough to marinate 1½ to 2 pounds
of flank steak or sirloin or
skin-on chicken parts

Teriyaki is probably most folks' introduction to Japanese cooking. This is a slightly spicier and updated interpretation of the classic. Sake is a fine Japanese rice wine. Mirin, a slightly sweeter and less alcoholic version used only for cooking, can be substituted, as can dry sherry.

⅓ *cup sake*
¼ *cup reduced-sodium soy sauce*
¼ *cup rice wine vinegar*
1 *tablespoon honey*
2 *tablespoons finely chopped fresh ginger*
1 *tablespoon toasted sesame oil*
1 *teaspoon dried hot red pepper flakes*
½ *teaspoon ground coriander*
2 *garlic cloves, minced*

In a small bowl, combine all ingredients. Place the beef or chicken in a shallow glass or ceramic dish. Add the marinade, turning to coat. Cover and refrigerate 2 to 6 hours for beef and 1 to 3 hours for chicken.

MARGARITA MARINADE

~ ~ ~ ~ ~ ~ ~ ~ ~

Makes about 1 cup; enough to marinate
1½ pounds of chicken or turkey breast cutlets,
jumbo or large peeled and deveined shrimp
or sea scallops, or swordfish

Inspired by the classic Mexican cocktail, this is a moderately spicy marinade that does justice to chicken or turkey cutlets, shrimp, sea scallops, or swordfish. I particularly like to grill a mix of marinated seafood threaded onto metal skewers alternating with cut-up bell peppers brushed with the marinade. The marinade also makes a good dipping sauce for grilled or steamed clams.

¼ cup fresh lime juice
¼ cup tequila
3 tablespoons triple sec
2 tablespoons vegetable oil
2 teaspoons grated lime zest
1½ teaspoons chili powder
1½ teaspoons sugar
½ teaspoon coarse salt, such as sea salt
1 or 2 jalapeño peppers, seeded and finely chopped

In a small bowl, combine all ingredients. Place poultry or seafood in a shallow glass or ceramic dish. Add the marinade, turning to coat. Cover and refrigerate, turning occasionally, about 1 hour for poultry and 30 minutes to 1 hour for seafood.

HUNT COUNTRY MARINADE

z z z z z z z z z

Makes about 1⅓ cups; enough to
marinate 2 ½ pounds of boneless venison,
beef, or lamb, 3 duck breasts, or 2 split game hens

Deep rich flavor and a tenderizer for boneless venison or beefsteak or small roasts as well as boneless leg of lamb, this contemporary version of a classic English marinade is also good for gamey poultry such as duck breasts and Cornish game hens.

¾ cup dry red wine
¼ cup balsamic vinegar
2 tablespoons extra-virgin olive oil
2 tablespoons molasses
3 garlic cloves, slivered
3 (2-inch) strips of orange peel
3 (2-inch) strips of lemon peel
8 whole cloves
8 whole peppercorns
2 bay leaves, broken in half
1 tablespoon crushed juniper berries or 2 tablespoons gin
2 tablespoons chopped fresh thyme or 2 teaspoons dried
2 tablespoons chopped fresh rosemary or 1½ teaspoon dried
½ teaspoon salt

In a small bowl, combine all ingredients. Place the meat or fowl in a shallow glass or ceramic dish. Add the marinade, turning to coat. Cover and refrigerate, turning occasionally, 6 to 24 hours for meat, and 1 to 3 hours for fowl.

SZECHUAN ORANGE
BEEF MARINADE

*Makes about 1 cup; enough to marinate
1½ pounds of beefsteak chunks*

Orange beef is a favorite in Chinese restaurants. This home version of the marinade is every bit as spicy and hot! Use boneless sirloin cut into 1½-inch chunks, then grill the marinated beef on bamboo skewers that have been soaked in water for about 10 minutes. Thread the orange peel from the marinade onto the skewers, as it will caramelize for a spicy/hot/sweet addition to the finished dish.

2 large seedless oranges
¼ cup rice wine vinegar
¼ cup reduced-sodium soy sauce
2 tablespoons chopped fresh ginger
1 tablespoon Asian hot sesame or chili oil
½ teaspoon dried hot red pepper flakes
2 garlic cloves, minced

Use a small knife to peel the oranges in long strips or spirals, taking care to cut only the colored portion and not the bitter white pith. Reserve the peel and squeeze ⅓ cup of juice from the oranges. In a small bowl, combine the orange peel and juice with the remaining ingredients. Place the beef in a shallow glass or ceramic dish. Add the marinade, stirring to coat. Cover and refrigerate, turning occasionally, 1 to 3 hours.

TEQUILA MOCKINGBIRD MARINADE

ꙅ ꙅ ꙅ ꙅ ꙅ ꙅ ꙅ ꙅ ꙅ

Makes about ¾ cup; enough to marinate 1 to 1½
pounds of boneless poultry or seafood

Inspired by the spicy food served at a neighborhood restaurant of the same name, we particularly like this for boneless chicken breasts or thighs, turkey cutlets, jumbo shrimp, and sea scallops. It is also a good sauce dabbed on grilled clams on the half shell.

¼ *cup corn oil*
3 *tablespoons lime juice*
3 *tablespoons tequila*
2 *tablespoons triple sec*
1½ *teaspoons grated lime zest*
1 *teaspoon chili powder*
1 *teaspoon sugar*
¼ *teaspoon coarse salt, such as sea salt*
1 *large jalapeño pepper, seeded and finely chopped*

In a small bowl, combine all ingredients. Let stand at least 15 minutes before using. (Can be made up to 1 day ahead and refrigerated.) Marinate chicken or turkey 1 to 3 hours in the refrigerator. Marinate peeled and deveined shrimp or scallops 30 minutes. Drain, but do not pat dry before grilling.

Sauces and Mops

〜 〜 〜 〜 〜 〜 〜 〜 〜

Pineapple Scotch Bonnet Tropical Heat ~ 68

Blackjack Bourbon Peach Sauce ~ 69

Spiced Apricot Walnut Sauce ~ 70

Marmalade Mustard Sauce ~ 71

Apricot Horseradish Sauce ~ 72

Big Sky Game Sauce ~ 73

Sausalito Herbed Wine Sauce ~ 74

Quick and Easy Off-the-Shelf Barbecue Sauce ~ 75

Pesto Brushing Sauce for Vegetables ~ 76

Double Jalapeño Glaze ~ 77

Red-Eye Glaze ~ 78

Backwagon Brisket Sauce ~ 79

Eagle Rock Ranch Sauce ~ 80

Kansas City Steak Sauce ~ 81

Sweet and Sour Fresh Plum and Coriander Sauce ~ 83

Bear Sauce ~ 84

Memphis Rib Sauce ~ 85

Sauces and Mops

A barbecue sauce is like the frosting on a cake. It makes a good thing even better. A sauce can work alone to enhance a simple grilled beefsteak or it can act in tandem with a marinade to finish off and complement the flavor imparted by the marinade. In fact, many barbecue sauces do double duty anyway. The sauce that is brushed on during grilling will caramelize and form a deliciously protective "crust" during those last minutes of grilling, but many sauces are also condiments and part of the recipe should be reserved to brush on after grilling or to be passed at the table.

Though almost all commercial barbecue sauces are tomato-based and usually quite thick and sweet (even though the sweetness can be masked by hickory flavoring or peppery spices), these kinds of sauces are but a drop in the barbecue bucket! I love tomato-based sauces for chicken and pork, but they have few uses on beefsteak and can completely overwhelm seafood and vegetables. Beef and veal barbecue sauces run the international gamut from variations on dark, rich Asian sauces using various highly spiced hoisin or soy sauce bases, to mustardy sauces that conjure up grilled steaks in France, Austria, Germany, or even England. Just as seafood itself ranges from delicate shellfish like scallops to assertive fish like bluefish or trout, so do the sauces that best complement them. A light wine and herb sauce can do wonders for shrimp, while a sauce heightens the flavor of bluefish. Sauces can even turn a simple grilled fruit into a fabulous side dish or memorable dessert.

While it is important to choose the right sauce for the desired result, it is equally important to understand what makes a barbecue sauce work.

Like the frosting on a cake, barbecue sauce forms a flavorful protective coating. If the food to be coated is low in fat, like seafood or skinless chicken, or if it is nonfat like vegetables or fruit, then the sauce should have at least a smidgen of oil to keep the food from sticking to the grill. These delicate kinds of foods are usually quick-cooking and thus the sauce can often be applied before and during the total grilling time.

For foods that take longer than 10 or 15 minutes to cook, and have their own protective skin or a higher fat content, the sauce should usually be applied during the last 10 or 15 minutes of cooking. The reason for this is that most barbecue sauces contain some sort of sugar, whether in the form of brown or granulated sugar, in liquids such as molasses, honey, or maple syrup, or in prepared ingredients such as ketchup or hoisin sauce. It is these sugars that caramelize to form a flavorful "crust" on barbecued foods. But this same rich brown caramelization can turn to blacked burned sugar after about 15 minutes of exposure to the intense heat of the grill. At the same time, it takes at least 5 minutes for the sugars to cook, so the window of tasty opportunity is rather slim for most barbecue sauces. But that indeed is the secret.

Because many barbecue sauces are so flavorful, they are often also used as table sauce for dipping or brushing on after cooking. The uncaramelized sugar provides a fresh counterpoint to the depth of flavor imparted by grilling. If you wish to use your sauce as both a barbecue sauce for meat, seafood, or poultry, and again as a condiment, be sure to set aside the condiment portion before grilling. Once a brush is used to dip both into the sauce and onto raw or partially cooked food, the brush and the sauce become a potential source of unwanted bacteria. If you wish to use this sauce later, boil it for at least 3 minutes first.

Most barbecue sauces keep rather well and can be made in advance. Store them tightly covered in the refrigerator, then return to room temperature or reheat gently before using.

PINEAPPLE
SCOTCH BONNET
TROPICAL HEAT

ι ι ι ι ι ι ι ι ι

*Makes about 2 cups; reserve ⅓ cup to use
as a table sauce and use the remainder
to sauce 2 pounds of chicken parts,
1 turkey breast, 2 pounds of pork chops,
2 duck breasts, 1½ pounds ham steaks,
or 1½ pounds tuna or swordfish steaks*

The natural sweetness of the pineapple and the sweet/sour mix of the chutney tame the heat of even the hottest pepper you dare to use in this lively sauce.

*1 tablespoon vegetable oil
1 or 2 Scotch bonnet or jalapeño peppers, seeded and minced
1 tablespoon curry powder
1 cup (8-ounce can) undrained crushed pineapple in juice
1 cup mango chutney, large pieces coarsely chopped
2 tablespoons fresh lime juice*

In a medium saucepan, heat the oil and cook the peppers and curry powder, stirring over medium-low heat, for 1 minute. Add the remaining ingredients and simmer, stirring often, until lightly thickened, about 10 minutes.

The sauce can be made up to 3 days ahead and refrigerated. Return to room temperature before brushing on during last 15 minutes of grilling. Gently warm reserved sauce and spoon over grilled food at the table.

BLACKJACK BOURBON
PEACH SAUCE

*Makes about 1¼ cups; enough to sauce
3 pounds of ribs, 2 pounds of drumsticks,
or 2 pounds of ham steaks*

This sweetly spiced sauce is just right for a slab of ribs, a heap of
drumsticks, or a hunk of ham. Tangy vinegar cole slaw and a mess
of fried onion rings complete this hearty plate. Finish with a few
hands of poker and the rest of the blackjack.

*¾ cup peach preserves
⅓ cup bourbon, preferably sour mash
⅓ cup raspberry or other fruit vinegar
1 tablespoon lemon juice
¾ teaspoon ground nutmeg
½ teaspoon ground cinnamon
¼ teaspoon salt
¼ teaspoon freshly ground pepper
¾ to 1 teaspoon hot pepper sauce*

In a small saucepan, combine all ingredients except hot pepper
sauce. Simmer over medium-low heat, stirring often, until lightly
thickened, about 10 minutes. Stir in the hot pepper sauce to taste.

The sauce can be made up to a month ahead and refrigerated.
Reheat before brushing on during the last 10 minutes of grilling.

SPICED APRICOT WALNUT SAUCE

ι ι ι ι ι ι ι ι ι

*Makes about 1½ cups; reserve ½ cup
to use as a table sauce and use
remainder as a grilling sauce for 1½ pounds
ham steaks or a 4-pound ham piece,
1 pound skinless, boneless chicken breasts
or thighs, 2 game hens, or 2 duck breasts*

In addition to its attributes as a sweet and sour sauce for ham or chicken, this is so good that I often serve it as a dipping sauce for fruit such as fresh pineapple spears or apple slices.

*1 cup canned or bottled apricot nectar
¼ cup fresh lemon juice
3 tablespoons grainy Dijon mustard
2 tablespoons walnut oil
½ teaspoon ground cardamom
⅛ teaspoon ground cloves
⅓ cup chopped toasted walnuts*

In a small saucepan, gently boil the nectar over medium heat until reduced by about one third, about 5 minutes. Stir in the lemon juice, mustard, oil, cardamom, and cloves. Reduce the heat to medium-low and simmer for 10 minutes. Stir in the nuts.

The sauce can be prepared up to 1 week ahead and refrigerated, but do not add the nuts until ready to use. Reheat gently to use as a table sauce or to brush on during last 10 minutes of grilling.

MARMALADE MUSTARD SAUCE

ꛥ ꛥ ꛥ ꛥ ꛥ ꛥ ꛥ ꛥ ꛥ

*Makes about 1½ cups; reserve ½ cup to use as a
table sauce and use remainder as a grilling
sauce for 1 pound of tuna, halibut, or swordfish
steaks, 1½ pounds of boneless pork chops,
1½ pounds of chicken drumsticks, or 2 duck breasts*

The combination of orange, anise, mustard, and rosemary is particularly well suited to seafood, but the sauce is also complementary to pork, dark meat of poultry, and especially lamb chops.

¾ teaspoon anise seeds
½ cup orange marmalade
½ cup Dijon mustard
⅓ cup fresh orange juice
¼ cup white wine vinegar
2 tablespoons chopped fresh rosemary or 2 teaspoons dried
1 teaspoon grated orange zest

Toss the anise seeds in a small skillet set over medium heat until fragrant and color begins to darken, about 2 minutes. Immediately remove from pan to prevent burning. Let the seeds cool, then coarsely crush them with a mortar and pestle or by placing in a heavy plastic sandwich bag and pounding with a meat mallet or rolling pin.

In a small saucepan, combine the remaining ingredients. Stir in the anise, then simmer over medium-low heat, stirring often, until lightly thickened, about 8 minutes.

The sauce can be made up to a week ahead. Reheat gently to use as a table sauce. Return to room temperature to brush on during the last 10 minutes of grilling.

APRICOT HORSERADISH SAUCE

Makes about 2 ½ cups; reserve 1 cup to use
as a table sauce and use remainder as a grilling sauce for
1½ pounds of skinless chicken breasts, thighs, or drumsticks,
2 pork tenderloins, or 2 pounds of boneless pork chops

Try this with dried figs or even prunes or a combination of dried fruits. The thick smoothness of the sauce makes it a flavorful, fat-free protective coating for skinless poultry.

½ cup chopped dried apricots (about 2 ounces)
1 cup dry white wine plus up to ¼ cup additional as needed
½ teaspoon powdered mustard, preferably Chinese mustard powder
¼ cup hoisin sauce
¼ cup ketchup
2 tablespoons grated fresh or prepared horseradish
1 tablespoon rice wine vinegar
¼ teaspoon dried hot pepper flakes

In a medium saucepan, combine the apricots and wine. Bring to a simmer over medium heat, then remove from heat and cover the pan. Let stand until the apricots are very soft, about 20 minutes. Puree in a food processor, then return to the pan. You should have a thick, but pourable puree. If necessary, add up to ¼ cup wine to achieve the pourable consistency. Add the remaining ingredients and simmer, uncovered, over medium-low heat for 10 minutes.

The sauce can be made up to 2 weeks ahead and refrigerated. Reheat gently to use as a table sauce or to brush on during the last 15 minutes of grilling time.

Big Sky Game Sauce

~ ~ ~ ~ ~ ~ ~ ~ ~

*Makes about 2 ½ cups; enough to sauce 3 pounds of
boneless venison or beefsteak or 4 pounds of pork chops*

The chiles and dried tomatoes are the secret to this assertive sauce
that is my husband's taste memory of a grilled venison he once had
during a camping trip to the big sky country of Montana.

3 dried ancho chiles
¼ cup oil-packed sun-dried tomatoes
4 garlic cloves, peeled and halved
1 onion, coarsely chopped
1 bay leaf, broken in half
1 tablespoon dried oregano
2 cups beef broth, preferably reduced-sodium
1 tablespoon dark brown sugar
3 tablespoons tomato paste
2 tablespoons red wine vinegar

In a medium saucepan, place the chiles, tomatoes, garlic, onion,
bay leaf, oregano, and broth. Cover and bring to a simmer over
medium-low heat. Simmer until the chiles are softened and vegetables
are tender, 12 to 15 minutes. Remove the bay leaf, then puree the
chile mixture in a food processor. Add the brown sugar and process
about 15 seconds to dissolve it, then add the tomato paste and vinegar. Process briefly to blend. Return the sauce to the saucepan and
simmer, uncovered, over medium-low heat for 5 minutes.

The sauce can be made up to a week ahead and refrigerated.
Return to room temperature for brushing on during the last 30
minutes of grilling.

SAUSALITO HERBED
WINE SAUCE

ι ι ι ι ι ι ι ι ι

*Makes about 1 cup; enough to sauce
1 pound of large or jumbo peeled and deveined shrimp,
1 pound of tuna, swordfish, or salmon steaks,
or 1 pound of skinless, boneless chicken breasts*

Though dried herbes de Provence, a commercial blend of several savory herbs, is called for, you can easily substitute any dried herb of choice such as tarragon, oregano, thyme, or marjoram. Don't bother with fresh herbs, since the more intense flavor imparted by dried is preferable here. This light sauce is typical of a California seafood treatment.

*1 tablespoon olive oil, preferably extra-virgin
3 tablespoons minced shallots
2 tablespoons Dijon mustard
⅔ cup dry white wine
1 tablespoon dried herbes de Provence
½ teaspoon freshly ground pepper
¼ teaspoon salt*

In a small saucepan, heat the oil and cook the shallots over medium-low heat for 1 minute. Stir in the mustard, then add the wine, herbes de Provence, pepper, and salt. Simmer gently for 5 minutes.

The sauce can be made up to 3 days ahead and refrigerated. Return to room temperature before using. Brush on before and during grilling.

QUICK AND EASY OFF-THE-SHELF BARBECUE SAUCE

ℰ ℰ ℰ ℰ ℰ ℰ ℰ ℰ ℰ

Makes about 2 cups; enough to sauce
3 pounds of pork ribs or chops or chicken parts
or 2 pounds of burgers

This is a very versatile recipe for how to make barbecue sauce from what you have in the pantry. Add a dash of other flavorings of choice if you have them, too. Soy sauce, prepared mustard, or even bottled steak sauce give a different twist to the basic recipe.

1½ tablespoons chili powder or more to taste
1 cup ketchup
1 cup bottled chili sauce
¼ cup Worcestershire sauce
¼ cup cider or any other vinegar

In a medium saucepan, heat the chili powder over medium heat, stirring just until fragrant, about 1 minute. Immediately add ¼ cup of water, then add the ketchup, chili sauce, Worcestershire, and vinegar. Simmer, partially covered, over medium-low heat until lightly thickened, about 20 minutes.

The sauce can be made up to 1 month ahead and refrigerated. Return to room temperature to brush on during last 15 minutes of grilling.

PESTO BRUSHING SAUCE
FOR VEGETABLES

ι ι ι ι ι ι ι ι ι

Makes about ¼ cup; enough to sauce
1 pound of sliced eggplant, zucchini, summer squash,
tomatoes, asparagus, or onions or a 1-pound loaf
of French bread, sliced and grilled

Because they are naturally fat-free, vegetables need a little oil to protect them from the heat of the grill. I've used herb-flavored oil successfully and have loved the lightly charred flavor of the fresh herbs. But this wonderfully rich version, which is almost a pesto, is my absolute favorite sauce for veggies, especially when they are to be the main course. Use it also for a dipping sauce for grilled Italian breads. If you have an abundance of basil and parsley in the garden, make the sauce and freeze it to grill summery tasting vegetables all winter long.

¼ *cup lightly packed basil leaves*
¼ *cup lightly packed flat-leaf parsley sprigs*
2 *tablespoons pine nuts*
5 *fresh sage leaves or ¾ teaspoon dried leaf sage*
2 *shallots, peeled and quartered*
3 *garlic cloves, peeled*
½ *cup olive oil*
3 *tablespoons fresh lemon juice*

Place the basil, parsley, pine nuts, and sage in a food processor. With the motor running, drop the shallots and garlic through the feed tube. Process until finely chopped, about 30 seconds. With the motor running, pour in the olive oil and lemon juice, and process to make a coarse puree, about 15 seconds.

The sauce can be made and refrigerated for up to 4 days or frozen up to 6 months. Return to room temperature to brush on vegetables before and during grilling.

DOUBLE JALAPEÑO GLAZE

ι ι ι ι ι ι ι ι ι

Makes about 1¼ cups; enough to sauce
2 pounds of chicken parts or 2 game hens

The juxtaposition of sweet jelly and fiery peppers is a brilliant idea that has many uses from a topper for bagels to an icing for a cream cheese and cracker snack. It also makes a shiny glaze for chicken or game hens. Different brands vary in heat intensity, but the addition of extra jalapeño and peppery chopped mint adds character.

1 cup jalapeño jelly
¼ cup dry white wine
1 tablespoon white wine vinegar
¼ cup chopped fresh mint
1 pickled jalapeño, finely chopped

In a small saucepan, heat the jelly, wine, and vinegar over low heat, stirring often, until the jelly is melted. Stir in the mint and jalapeño. Take the pan off the heat and steep for at least 30 minutes before using.

The sauce can be made up to 3 days ahead and refrigerated. Reheat gently before brushing on during the last 15 minutes of grilling.

RED-EYE GLAZE

~ ~ ~ ~ ~ ~ ~ ~ ~

Makes about 1 cup; enough to sauce
1½ pounds of ham steaks, a 3-pound
boneless ham, or 2 pork tenderloins

Red-eye gravy is a classic Southern sauce for ham. The secret ingredient is coffee, and it makes all the difference in a glaze for grilled ham, too.

1 cup packed light or dark brown sugar
¼ cup pommery mustard
¼ cup cider vinegar
¼ cup strong coffee or 1 tablespoon instant coffee dissolved in ¼
  cup hot water
¾ teaspoon coarsely ground pepper

In a small saucepan, combine all ingredients. Stir over low heat until sugar is dissolved. Raise heat to medium-low and simmer for 5 minutes, stirring often.

The sauce can be made up to a week ahead and refrigerated. Reheat gently before brushing on during last 10 minutes of grilling.

BACKWAGON BRISKET SAUCE

ι ι ι ι ι ι ι ι ι

Makes about 2 ½ cups; reserve 2 cups to use
as a table sauce, and use remainder to brush
on 3 pounds of brisket or boneless beefsteak

Texans don't brush sauce on brisket during grilling. Instead, the sauce is offered on the side to slather on after slicing. I generally agree with Texans, but do like to give the brisket one quick brush about 15 minutes before I take it off the grill. The lightly caramelized glaze or crust is a nice counterpoint to the spooned-on sauce. I also like to reheat barbecued brisket in the sauce to use for barbecued sandwich fillings.

2 tablespoons vegetable oil
1 medium onion, chopped
1 celery rib, chopped
2 garlic cloves, minced
1½ tablespoons chili powder
1½ tablespoons brown sugar
2 teaspoons dried leaf oregano
1½ teaspoons paprika
1 bay leaf, broken in half
¾ cup reduced-sodium beef broth
½ cup ketchup
½ cup bottled chili sauce
¼ cup cider vinegar
2 tablespoons Worcestershire sauce
½ teaspoon hot pepper sauce, or more to taste

(continued)

In a medium saucepan, heat the oil and sauté the onion, celery, and garlic over medium heat until just softened, about 4 minutes. Stir in the chili powder and cook for 30 seconds. Stir in the sugar, oregano, paprika, and bay leaf. Add the broth, ketchup, chili sauce, vinegar, and Worcestershire. Bring just to a boil, then reduce heat to medium-low and simmer, uncovered, until lightly thickened, about 25 minutes. Add the hot pepper sauce.

The sauce can be made up to a month in advance and refrigerated. Return to room temperature before brushing on during last 20 minutes of grilling.

EAGLE ROCK RANCH SAUCE

Makes about 3 cups; enough to sauce
4 pounds of brisket or beef roast or steaks or a
4- to 5-pound boneless leg of lamb or pork roast

This multifaceted sauce is named in honor of a friend and fellow food writer who lives a multifaceted life on Eagle Rock Ranch in Wyoming. Though I developed the recipe to use on brisket or barbecued chuck roast, my family loves it with sliced leg of lamb or shaved barbecued pork butt.

1 tablespoon peanut oil
1 medium onion, chopped
2 garlic cloves, minced
1 cup chopped fresh tomato
½ cup chicken broth, preferably reduced-sodium
½ cup orange juice
½ cup rice wine vinegar
¼ cup chopped pimiento

2 tablespoons soy sauce
2 tablespoons toasted sesame oil
1 tablespoon fresh lime juice
1 tablespoon honey
1 tablespoon minced fresh ginger

In a medium saucepan, heat the peanut oil and cook the onion and garlic over medium heat until just softened, about 4 minutes. Stir in the remaining ingredients, bring just to a boil, then reduce the heat to medium-low and simmer until slightly thickened, about 25 minutes.

The sauce can be made up to a month ahead and refrigerated. Return to room temperature to brush on during the last 30 minutes of grilling or to use as simmering sauce for leftover sliced barbecued beef, lamb, or pork.

KANSAS CITY
STEAK SAUCE

*Makes about 3 cups; enough to sauce
3 pounds of boneless beefsteak or 5 pounds
of chicken parts, ribs, or burgers*

Every region has its specialty, and Kansas City has long been known for its prize steaks. Although a good piece of meat, properly grilled, actually needs no embellishment, this steak sauce is like the frosting on a cake—making it just a little bit more special! I like to make it in large batches, then keep it in the refrigerator to use as a sauce for barbecued chicken, steak, or ribs, or as a "ketchup" on burgers, too.

(continued)

2 tablespoons vegetable oil
1 medium onion, finely chopped
1 celery rib, finely chopped
2 teaspoons anise seeds, lightly crushed with a rolling pin
1 teaspoon celery seeds
1 tablespoon dry mustard
1 cup ketchup
1 cup bottled chili sauce
¼ cup apple cider or apple juice
3 tablespoons cider vinegar
2 tablespoons Worcestershire sauce
2 tablespoons honey

In a medium saucepan, heat the oil and cook the onion and celery over medium heat until softened, about 5 minutes. Add the anise seeds and cook, stirring, for 1 minute. Add the celery seeds and cook, stirring, for 30 seconds. Stir in the mustard until dissolved, then stir in the remaining ingredients. Bring to a boil, then reduce the heat to medium-low and simmer until lightly thickened, 15 to 20 minutes.

The sauce can be made up to a month ahead and refrigerated. Return to room temperature before brushing on during last 20 minutes of grilling.

Sweet and Sour
Fresh Plum and
Coriander Sauce

乁 乁 乁 乁 乁 乁 乁 乁 乁

Makes about 2 ½ cups; enough to sauce
4 pounds of pork ribs or chicken parts or 3 pounds
of burgers or boneless steaks

Use any ripe, juicy plum for this sauce. Grating ginger seems to accentuate its sharpness more than chopping, and here it nicely balances the sweet plums and ginger ale. Though the ingredients may read a bit exotic for an all-purpose barbecue sauce, this is really terrific with nearly everything from burgers to pork ribs.

2 tablespoons vegetable oil
1 medium onion, finely chopped
2 garlic cloves, minced
1 tablespoon grated fresh ginger
1 cup bottled chili sauce
1 cup ginger ale
2 tablespoons rice wine vinegar
1½ tablespoons soy sauce
1 cup chopped pitted plums
¼ cup chopped fresh cilantro

In a medium saucepan, heat the oil and cook the onion and garlic over medium heat until softened, about 5 minutes. Add the ginger and stir for 30 seconds, then add the remaining ingredients except cilantro. Bring just to a boil, then reduce the heat to medium-low and simmer, uncovered, until lightly thickened, about 25 minutes. Stir in the cilantro and simmer an additional 5 minutes.

The sauce can be made up to a month ahead and refrigerated. Return to room temperature to brush on during the last 20 minutes of grilling.

BEAR SAUCE

ι ι ι ι ι ι ι ι ι

Makes about 4 cups; enough to sauce 6 pounds
of beef, venison, or bear steaks

Large lean cuts of meat, like bear, should be grilled over an indirect fire for a long, slow cooking to tenderize and infuse with smokiness. To keep the bear from drying out, baste it often with this sauce. If you don't happen to have any bear to barbecue, it's also good on venison or beef.

2 cups beef broth, preferably reduced-sodium
1 cup red wine
⅓ cup Worcestershire sauce
2 tablespoons red wine vinegar
1 cup thick bottled hickory-flavored barbecue sauce
1 teaspoon hot pepper sauce, or more to taste

In a medium saucepan, bring all ingredients to a boil. Reduce the heat to medium-low and simmer, uncovered, until lightly thickened, 35 to 45 minutes. The sauce will still be rather thin for a barbecue sauce.

The sauce can be made up to a month ahead and refrigerated. Return to room temperature before brushing on during last 45 minutes of grilling.

MEMPHIS RIB SAUCE

~ ~ ~ ~ ~ ~ ~ ~ ~

*Makes about 4 cups; reserve 2 cups to brush on
after grilling, and use remainder to brush on 4 pounds
of pork ribs or pork steaks during grilling*

Memphis is the town where Elvis is king. That is, of course, unless
you are a rib fancier. Then you really know what is king—and it is
any of the legendary rib places in town. Drop by for a slab after
you see Graceland. Note that real Memphis ribs are barbecued with
a spicy dry rub, then the sauce is slathered on at the very end, or
even after cooking. Look for canned or bottled chipotles in adobo
sauce in Latin American groceries or in the Latin food section of
large supermarkets. The sauce lends a smoky/hot flavor to the barbecue sauce that is incomparable, but if you can't find it, use 1
tablespoon of chili powder stirred into 2 tablespoons of ketchup.

*1 tablespoon vegetable oil
4 garlic cloves, minced
3 ½ cups (28-ounce can) crushed tomatoes in puree
½ cup molasses
½ cup beer
¼ cup cider vinegar
2 tablespoons Worcestershire sauce
2 tablespoons chipotles in adobo sauce
1 teaspoon ground allspice
½ teaspoon ground cinnamon
¼ teaspoon ground cloves*

In a large saucepan, combine all ingredients and bring just to a

(continued)

boil. Reduce the heat to medium-low and simmer, uncovered, until moderately thick, about 30 minutes.

The sauce can be made up to a month ahead and refrigerated. Return to room temperature to use as a table sauce or to brush on during last 10 minutes of grilling.

SESAME HOISIN SAUCE

Makes about 1½ cups; enough to sauce 1½ pounds of boneless beefsteak or tuna steak or 2 pounds of shoulder or rib lamb chops

Rich and thick and dark, this sauce gives a distinctly Chinese flavor to beefsteak, especially flank steak, and to tuna steaks. It is also terrific on lamb chops, particularly to dress up the less expensive shoulder chops.

3 to 5 dried red chiles, broken in pieces
4 slices of fresh ginger
2 large garlic cloves, sliced
3 star anise
½ cup reduced-sodium soy sauce
½ cup hoisin sauce
¼ cup rice wine vinegar
2 tablespoons toasted sesame oil

Tie the chiles, ginger, cloves, and anise together in a piece of cheesecloth or in a spice bag. In a small saucepan, place the spice bag, remaining ingredients, and ½ cup water. Bring just to a boil, then partially cover the pan and reduce the heat to medium-low. Simmer until lightly thickened, about 20 minutes. Let the spice bag cool in the sauce, then remove and discard it.

The sauce can be made up to 2 weeks ahead and refrigerated. Return to room temperature to brush on during the last 10 minutes of grilling.

Hibachi Steak House Sauce

*Makes about 1¼ cups; reserve about ½ cup
to serve at the table, and use remainder to brush
on 1½ pounds of boneless beefsteak, tuna or
swordfish steaks, or jumbo peeled and deveined shrimp*

Admittedly, this isn't an authentic recipe for Japanese steak sauce, but it tastes a lot like one served in my favorite Japanese steak house. I like to brush some on during grilling, then serve the rest to brush on at the table. If you like flank steak, which benefits from a bit of tenderizing, use half of the sauce to marinate the meat overnight in the refrigerator, then use the remainder as a brushing sauce.

½ cup dry sherry
½ cup reduced-sodium soy sauce
2 tablespoons molasses
2 tablespoons rice wine vinegar
4 garlic cloves, minced
2 tablespoons minced fresh ginger
⅛ teaspoon crushed hot pepper flakes
1 tablespoon cornstarch dissolved in 3 tablespoons cold water

In a small saucepan, combine all ingredients except cornstarch mixture. Bring just to a boil, then reduce the heat to medium-low, and simmer, uncovered, for 10 minutes. Stir in the cornstarch mixture and return to a boil. Cook, stirring, for 1 minute until thickened.

The sauce can be made up to a week ahead and refrigerated. Reheat gently to use as a table sauce and return to room temperature to brush on during last 10 minutes of grilling.

ASIAN BLACK BEAN
AND ORANGE SAUCE

ﾟ ﾟ ﾟ ﾟ ﾟ ﾟ ﾟ ﾟ ﾟ

*Makes about 1 cup; enough to sauce 1 pound
of boneless beefsteak or tuna steak
or 1½ pounds of lamb chops*

Based on bottled black bean sauce, this is quick and easy to make
and does wonders for steaks and seafood.

*½ cup bottled black bean sauce
½ cup orange juice
2 tablespoons rice wine vinegar
2 garlic cloves, minced
1 teaspoon grated orange zest
1 teaspoon cornstarch dissolved in 1½ teaspoons cold water*

In a small saucepan, combine all ingredients except the cornstarch mixture. Bring just to a boil, then reduce the heat to
medium-low and simmer for 5 minutes. Return to a boil and
whisk in the cornstarch mixture. Cook, stirring, for 1 minute until
thickened.

The sauce can be made up to a week ahead and refrigerated.
Reheat gently to use as a table sauce or to brush on during the last
10 minutes of grilling.

HERBAL BALSAMIC GLAZE

ɀ ɀ ɀ ɀ ɀ ɀ ɀ ɀ ɀ

*Makes about 1 cup; enough to glaze 1½ pounds
of tuna or swordfish steak, 1 pound of jumbo
or large peeled and deveined shrimp, or 1½ pounds
of skinless, boneless chicken breasts*

Good balsamic vinegar is almost like sippin' whiskey. It's far less acidic than other vinegars, and thus needs very little oil to balance it in a vinaigrette. In this glaze, I've added nothing more than a touch of wine and sugar and any fresh herb that you like. Add half of the herbs during cooking to infuse the glaze, then stir in the remainder afterward for a fresher flavor.

1 cup balsamic vinegar
⅓ cup dry white wine
2 tablespoons sugar
1 tablespoon olive oil
2 tablespoons chopped fresh thyme
2 tablespoons chopped fresh tarragon
1½ tablespoons green peppercorns, lightly crushed

In a small saucepan, combine the vinegar, wine, sugar, oil, and half each of the thyme, tarragon, and peppercorns. Bring just to a boil, then reduce the heat to medium-low and simmer until lightly thickened, about 15 minutes. Stir in the remaining thyme, tarragon, and peppercorns.

The sauce can be made up to a week ahead and refrigerated. Return to room temperature before using. Brush on during the last 15 minutes of grilling.

THAI RIB SAUCE

ι ι ι ι ι ι ι ι ι

*Makes about 1¼ cups; enough to sauce 4 pounds
of pork ribs or pork chops, 3 pounds of
chicken parts, or 3 game hens*

Because this is relatively high in sugar and thus tends to burn,
brush it on only during the last 10 minutes of cooking to make a
shiny, caramelized glaze. If you wish a hotter flavor, sprinkle the
ribs with cayenne before grilling.

¼ cup sugar
1 tablespoon cornstarch
1¼ cups chicken broth, preferably reduced-sodium
½ cup rice wine vinegar
3 tablespoons Thai fish sauce (nam pla)
2 tablespoons minced fresh ginger
*2 tablespoons chopped lemongrass or 1 teaspoon
    grated lemon zest*
½ teaspoon crushed hot pepper flakes
2 tablespoons finely chopped fresh basil

In a small saucepan, stir together the sugar and cornstarch.
Whisk in the broth, vinegar, fish sauce, ginger, lemongrass, and
pepper flakes. Bring to a boil, stirring constantly, and then cook
until lightly thickened, about 1 minute. Reduce heat and simmer 2
to 3 minutes. Remove from heat and stir in the basil.

The sauce can be made up to 1 week ahead and refrigerated.
Return to room temperature before brushing on during last 10
minutes of grilling.

SAN ANTONIO SAUCE

Makes about 2 ½ cups; enough to sauce 4 pounds
of steak or brisket, 4 pounds of chicken parts,
or 4 pounds of pork chops or pork steaks

Germans, Italians, French, Mexicans, and Native Americans have all contributed greatly to the food culture that is San Antonio. In fact, a German family has for years manufactured the area's best-known chili powder. This is an all-purpose barbecue sauce with a south-central Texas twang.

1 tablespoon vegetable oil
1 small onion, minced
2 garlic cloves, minced
1½ tablespoons chili powder
1½ cups tomato sauce
1 cup beer
1 can (4 ounces) chopped green chiles
¼ cup molasses
¼ cup cider vinegar

In a medium saucepan, heat the oil and sauté the onion over medium heat until softened, about 5 minutes. Add the garlic and chili powder and cook, stirring, for 1 minute. Add the tomato sauce, beer, chiles, molasses, and vinegar. Bring to a boil, then reduce the heat to medium-low, and simmer, uncovered, until lightly thickened, about 20 minutes.

The sauce can be made up to a month ahead and refrigerated. Return to room temperature before brushing on during last 15 minutes of grilling.

MOLE BARBECUE SAUCE

{ { { { { { { { {

*Makes about 3 ½ cups; enough to sauce a 10-pound
turkey, 2 turkey breasts, 6 pounds of chicken parts
or pork chops, or 7 pounds of pork spareribs*

Mole, the complex sauce made famous by some Mexican nuns
who had to whip up a poultry dish from the pantry for unexpected
visiting clerics, is here simplified and interpreted for unexpected
American guests, clerics or not.

3 tablespoons vegetable oil
1 large onion, chopped
2 garlic cloves, minced
2 tablespoons chili powder
1 teaspoon ground cumin
1 teaspoon dried oregano
½ teaspoon ground coriander
½ teaspoon ground cinnamon
¼ teaspoon cayenne pepper
⅛ teaspoon ground cloves
2 cups chicken broth, preferably reduced-sodium
1¾ cups tomato sauce
1 can (4 ounces) chopped green chiles
2 tablespoons red wine vinegar
2 tablespoons chopped almonds
2 tablespoons raisins
½ ounce unsweetened chocolate

In a medium saucepan, heat the oil and sauté the onion over medium heat until softened, about 5 minutes. Add the garlic and chili powder and cook, stirring, for 1 minute. Stir in the cumin, oregano, coriander, cinnamon, cayenne, and cloves. Then add the broth, tomato sauce, chiles, vinegar, almonds, raisins, and chocolate. Bring just to a boil, then reduce the heat to medium-low and simmer, uncovered, until thickened to a chili sauce consistency, about 30 minutes.

The sauce can be made up to a month ahead and refrigerated. Return to room temperature to brush on during the last 30 minutes of grilling.

MOONSHINE MADNESS

*Makes about 1¼ cups; enough to sauce 3 pounds
of pork spareribs or pork chops or chicken parts*

Easier than making moonshine, and also quite legal, this sauce gives a kick to pork and chicken.

½ cup bottled chili sauce
½ cup bourbon whiskey
3 tablespoons Dijon mustard
3 tablespoons reduced-sodium soy sauce

In a small saucepan, bring all ingredients just to a boil. Reduce the heat to medium-low and simmer, uncovered, until lightly thickened, about 15 minutes.

The sauce can be made up to a month ahead and refrigerated. Before using return it to room temperature. Brush on during last 15 minutes of grilling.

DARJEELING BRUSH

*Makes about 1½ cups; enough to sauce 3 pounds
of chicken parts, pork chops, or burgers*

Tea is a terrific cooking ingredient, especially in barbecue sauces
where it lends a distinctive flavor. Brush the thin sauce liberally on
chicken or game hens or pork chops to keep them moist and well
flavored during grilling.

1 tablespoon peanut oil
¼ cup minced shallots
2 teaspoons curry powder
1 cup strong tea
⅓ cup fresh lemon juice
¼ cup honey
1 tablespoon tomato paste
½ teaspoon crushed hot pepper flakes

In a small saucepan, heat the oil and sauté the shallots over
medium heat until softened, about 2 minutes. Stir in the curry
powder and cook for 30 seconds. Add the tea, lemon juice, honey,
tomato paste, and pepper flakes. Bring just to a boil, then reduce
the heat to medium-low and simmer, stirring often, until lightly
thickened, about 30 minutes.

The sauce can be made up to 2 weeks ahead and refrigerated.
Return to room temperature to brush on during last 15 minutes of
grilling.

RED HOT HELLFIRE
AND DAMNATION
MOPPIN' SAUCE

ı ı ı ı ı ı ı ı ı

*Makes about 2 cups; enough to sauce 4 pounds
of chicken parts, pork spareribs, or pork chops*

This is a revival meeting for your taste buds. Don't try it unless
you are willing to repent and have a sugary dessert afterward to
tame the demons on your tongue. The brand of hot sauce deter-
mines the degree of heat. Start with a mild one, and work your
way up.

2 tablespoons olive oil
1 small green pepper, finely chopped
1 small onion, finely chopped
2 garlic cloves, minced
¾ cup red hot sauce, such as Durkee's
¾ cup carbonated lemon-lime beverage or ginger ale
¼ cup honey

In a medium saucepan, heat the oil and sauté the green pepper
and onion until softened, about 5 minutes. Add the garlic and
cook for 1 minute. Add the hot sauce, carbonated beverage, and
honey. Bring just to a boil, then reduce the heat and simmer,
uncovered, until lightly thickened, about 15 minutes.

The sauce can be made up to a week ahead and refrigerated.
Return to room temperature to brush on during the last 10 minutes of grilling.

MAPLE APPLE
MOPPIN' SAUCE

~ ~ ~ ~ ~ ~ ~ ~ ~

Makes about 3 cups; enough to sauce 5 pounds
of chicken parts or 4 game hens

Take this to an autumn grilling tailgate party to brush on chicken.
Round out the grilling menu with a thermos of hot beef broth, a
wild rice salad, oatmeal cookies, and crisp apples. That's enough
fuel to win any game.

2 tablespoons vegetable oil
1 medium onion, finely chopped
1 celery rib, finely chopped
1½ teaspoons dried leaf sage
⅔ cup maple syrup
½ cup bottled chili sauce
½ cup apple cider
½ cup cider vinegar
2 tablespoons reduced-sodium soy sauce
1 teaspoon hot pepper sauce

In a medium saucepan, heat the oil and sauté the onion and
celery over medium heat until softened, about 5 minutes. Stir in
the sage, then add the maple syrup, chili sauce, cider, vinegar, and
soy sauce. Bring just to a boil, then reduce the heat to medium-low
and simmer, uncovered, until lightly thickened, about 25 minutes.
Stir in the hot pepper sauce.

The sauce can be made up to 2 weeks ahead and refrigerated.
Return to room temperature to brush on during the last 15 minutes of grilling.

LIME RICKEY SAUCE

ૅ ૅ ૅ ૅ ૅ ૅ ૅ ૅ ૅ

*Makes about 1 cup; enough to sauce 3 pounds
of lamb chops, 2 pounds of skinless, boneless chicken
breasts or thighs, or 2 pounds of pork chops*

This is fine with fresh lime juice, but I like it even better with the lightly sweetened bottled Rose's Lime Juice, found in the drink-making section of the market. It just seems to go better with the gin. This is a good sauce for chicken and pork, but is especially well suited to lamb chops.

½ cup lime marmalade
¼ cup prepared horseradish
3 tablespoons Rose's Lime Juice or fresh lime juice
2 tablespoons white wine Worcestershire sauce
2 tablespoons gin
1 tablespoon white wine vinegar
1 teaspoon grated lime zest

In a small saucepan, combine all ingredients. Bring just to a boil, then reduce the heat to medium-low and simmer, stirring often, for 5 minutes.

The sauce can be made up to a month ahead and refrigerated. Reheat gently to brush on during last 10 minutes of grilling.

SIMPLE SIMMERING SAUCE

*Makes about 4 cups sauce; reserve 3 cups
sauce for simmering and use remainder to brush
on 3 pounds of pork shoulder steaks or pork chops*

I like to brush some of this sauce on pork shoulder steaks during grilling, then simmer the grilled steaks in the remaining sauce on top of the stove until the meat is so tender that it literally falls off the bone. Pick out the bones, then ladle the pork and wonderfully savory sauce onto big soft rolls for barbecue sandwiches. For a real treat, spoon on some creamy cole slaw, too. I find that commercial hickory-flavored barbecue sauces have an overwhelming flavor, but as an ingredient in a homemade sauce, it lends just the right amount of smokiness.

2 cups bottled chili sauce
1½ cups beer
½ cup molasses
¼ cup hickory-flavored bottled barbecue sauce
¼ cup Worcestershire sauce
¼ cup cider vinegar
1 medium onion, finely chopped
2 garlic cloves, minced
1 teaspoon hot pepper sauce, or to taste

In a medium saucepan, bring all ingredients except hot pepper sauce to a boil. Reduce the heat to medium-low and simmer, uncovered, until lightly thickened, about 15 minutes. Stir in hot pepper sauce.

The sauce can be made up to 2 weeks ahead and refrigerated. Reheat to use as a simmering sauce or return to room temperature to brush on during the last 15 minutes of grilling.

SZECHUAN GARLIC BARBECUE SAUCE

ι ι ι ι ι ι ι ι ι

*Makes about 1 cup; reserve ½ cup for dipping
and brush remainder on 1 pound of skinless,
boneless chicken breasts or thinly
sliced boneless pork chops*

Brush some of the sauce on pork chops or boneless chicken during grilling, then slice the meat and serve on a bed of shredded lettuce with toothpicks to spear the meat or fowl and dip into more of the sauce. It's a great cocktail nibbler for a summer party.

6 tablespoons dry sherry
¼ cup reduced-sodium soy sauce
2 tablespoons rice wine vinegar
2 tablespoons bottled plum sauce
2 tablespoons hot chili paste or sauce
6 garlic cloves, minced

In a small bowl, combine all ingredients. Let stand at least 15 minutes or refrigerate up to 24 hours. Return to room temperature to use as a dipping sauce or to brush on before and during grilling.

SHOT AND A CHASER SAUCE

*Makes 2 cups; enough to brush on 3 pounds
of chicken parts or pork chops*

Double or triple this to use as the all-American barbecue sauce for ribs, pork chops, chicken, and even burgers. It will keep for weeks in the refrigerator. If you are doing ribs, mop them during the first half of cooking with a mix of 1 part cider vinegar to 10 parts water with a pinch of hot pepper flakes to keep them moist, then brush on the sauce near the end.

2 tablespoons vegetable oil
1 medium onion, finely chopped
2 garlic cloves, minced
1 cup bottled chili sauce
¾ cup beer
¼ cup molasses
3 tablespoons cider vinegar
3 tablespoons bourbon, preferably sour mash
1½ teaspoons Worcestershire sauce
½ teaspoon Tabasco or other hot pepper sauce

In a medium saucepan, heat the oil over medium heat and cook the onion and garlic, stirring often, until softened, about 5 minutes. Stir in the remaining ingredients except Tabasco. Simmer, uncovered, over medium-low heat until reduced to about 2 cups, 20 to 25 minutes. Stir in Tabasco.

The sauce can be made up to 1 month ahead and refrigerated. Return to room temperature before using. Brush on during the last 10 minutes of grilling.

～～

TRIPLE MUSTARD SAUCE

ᘡ ᘡ ᘡ ᘡ ᘡ ᘡ ᘡ ᘡ ᘡ

*Makes about ¾ cup; enough for 1 to 1½
pounds of meat or fish*

This is both a sauce and a condiment for beefsteak, lamb chops, burgers, and tuna steaks.

4 tablespoons Dijon mustard
1 teaspoon dry mustard, such as Coleman's
1 teaspoon mustard seeds
1 teaspoon cracked pepper
3 tablespoons brandy
2 tablespoons olive oil
1½ tablespoons tarragon or white wine vinegar
2 teaspoons honey
3 tablespoons chopped fresh tarragon or 2 teaspoons dried

In a small bowl, stir together the Dijon and dry mustards, mustard seeds, and pepper until dry mustard is dissolved. Stir in remaining ingredients. Let stand at least 15 minutes before using. (Can be made 3 days ahead and refrigerated.)

When ready to use, set aside ¼ cup mustard sauce. Use remainder to brush on liberally during last 7 to 10 minutes of cooking. Brush on reserved sauce as soon as meat or fish is removed from grill.

Aioli Vegetable Sauce

$\wr\ \wr\ \wr\ \wr\ \wr\ \wr\ \wr\ \wr\ \wr$

*Makes about 1 cup; enough to sauce 1 pound
of eggplant, peppers, tomatoes, summer squashes,
broccoli, or asparagus or a 1-pound loaf of sliced
French or Italian bread*

Mayonnaise, low-fat or regular, makes a wonderful base for a quick and easy barbecue sauce for vegetables and for grilled bread, too.

1 cup mayonnaise, low-fat or regular
1 tablespoon white wine vinegar
4 garlic cloves, minced
⅛ teaspoon crushed red pepper flakes

In a small mixing bowl, whisk together all of the ingredients. Refrigerate at least 2 hours to allow flavors to blend.

The sauce can be made up to 24 hours ahead and refrigerated. Brush on before and during grilling.

SWEET AND SPICY
GRILLED FRUIT SAUCE

ꙅ ꙅ ꙅ ꙅ ꙅ ꙅ ꙅ ꙅ ꙅ

Makes about ⅔ cup; enough sauce for 1 large
pineapple, 6 halved bananas, 8 slices of banana
bread or pound cake, or 4 apples or pears,
cut into rings

Not all fruits take well to grilling, but those that do are simply magnificent. Grilled pineapple rings with a scoop of vanilla ice cream or frozen yogurt spooned atop and a finish of warmed chocolate sauce is an incomparable dessert. Grilled bananas served on top of a grilled banana bread slice with a drizzling of rum is just as inspired. Grilled apple or pear slices served alongside grilled pork tenderloin elevates a simple autumnal grill into the memorable meal of the season. And these ideas are just the beginning.

¾ cup maple syrup
1 tablespoon butter
2 tablespoons lemon juice
½ teaspoon ground cinnamon
⅛ teaspoon ground nutmeg
⅛ teaspoon ground cloves

In a small saucepan, simmer the maple syrup over medium heat until reduced to ½ cup, about 10 minutes. Stir in the butter until melted, then remove from the heat and let cool. Stir in the lemon juice, cinnamon, nutmeg, and cloves.

The sauce can be made up to a week ahead and refrigerated. Heat to lukewarm to remelt the butter, then brush onto fruits or cake before and during grilling.

Rubs and Pastes

~ ~ ~ ~ ~ ~ ~ ~ ~ ~

Rubs and Pastes

Rubs and pastes are also referred to as dry marinades. A rub is a mixture of herbs and spices, and has no liquid. A paste is simply a rub that is moistened with a little aromatic liquid. Both are usually very potent, often peppery, and are designed to impart an assertive flavor to the food.

Dry rubs often rely on dried herbs and spices. For best results, these should be taken from relatively fresh jars that have been kept in a cool place out of direct sunlight for no more than 6 months. After that, dried herbs and spices begin to lose potency, and some may even develop unpleasant tastes. Dry rub combinations can themselves be stored in the spice cupboard for up to several months depending upon the freshness of the original ingredients.

Dry rubs make lovely gifts, especially when accompanied by a recipe for using them.

Some pastes are also made of dried herbs and spices, but others begin with crushed fresh herbs, citrus peels, and commercial liquid seasonings such as soy sauce. These pastes must be stored in the refrigerator, but most will remain flavorful for a day or two.

Because dry rubs and pastes completely cover the food, they also act as a protector during grilling. The raw rub or paste flavors the meat during the standing or marinating time, then the heat of the grill "cooks" the ingredients and they take on a toasted flavor that further enhances the grilled food. If the rub or paste contains sugar of any kind, it should be used on thinner cuts of food that take less than 15 minutes to cook. Otherwise, the sugars may burn.

TANDOOR RUB

〜 〜 〜 〜 〜 〜 〜 〜 〜

Makes about 3 tablespoons; enough to rub on
2 ½ pounds of chicken parts, 2 pounds of peeled
and deveined shrimp, or 2 ½ pounds of lamb chops

The characteristic golden yellow color comes from the turmeric, an underused spice that imparts a mild peppery flavor along with its lovely color. The Indian tandoor ovens turn out incredibly moist and juicy foods, particularly chicken. But a covered grill, medium heat, an aluminum foil pan of water set in the coals or on the rack to add some humidity to the air can do much the same thing.

1 teaspoon ground coriander
1 teaspoon ground ginger
1 teaspoon ground turmeric
1 teaspoon ground cumin
1 teaspoon paprika
1 teaspoon salt
½ teaspoon ground cardamom
½ teaspoon cayenne
2 garlic cloves, minced or 1 teaspoon garlic powder

In a small bowl, stir together the coriander, ginger, turmeric, cumin, paprika, salt, cardamom, and cayenne. If you are planning to use the rub immediately, add the minced garlic. If you would like to store the rub up to 1 month in a tightly covered container, use the garlic powder, or add the fresh garlic when you are ready to cook.

Smear the rub onto the surface of the chicken, shrimp, or lamb, and let stand at room temperature for 15 minutes or refrigerate up to 2 hours before grilling.

Autumn Herb Rub

ι ι ι ι ι ι ι ι ι

*Makes about 3 tablespoons; enough to rub on 2 ½ pounds of turkey
breast steaks, 4 pounds of turkey drumsticks, or 4 game hens*

The classic herb combination can bring the smells and flavors of
Thanksgiving to grilled turkey steaks or drumsticks, and makes a
mini-holiday supper when applied to game hens. Note that rubbed
sage and thyme are preferred over dried leaf herbs for their smooth
texture here, but be sure that the container is fresh so the herbs
have retained their potency.

4 teaspoons dried rubbed sage
2 teaspoons dried rubbed thyme
2 teaspoons dried savory
1 teaspoon salt
1 teaspoon coarsely ground black pepper

In a small bowl, combine all of the ingredients. Use immediately or store in a tightly covered container for up to 1 month.
Rub on the surface of the turkey or game hens, then let stand for
15 minutes at room temperature or refrigerate up to 4 hours
before grilling.

UPTOWN CREOLE RUB

ζ ζ ζ ζ ζ ζ ζ ζ ζ

*Makes about ¼ cup; enough to rub on 3 pounds
of sea scallops, 3 pounds of turkey or chicken burgers,
or 3 pounds of boneless skinless chicken breasts*

Creole cooking sometimes fancies itself to be more "uptown" than its cousin, Cajun cooking. While it may have a bit more complexity in its origins, both are eminently worthy eating. This rub is more mildly spiced than the Downtown Cajun Rub, so is well suited to more delicate foods.

*2 ½ tablespoons paprika
2 teaspoons ground white pepper
2 teaspoons dried oregano
2 teaspoons dried leaf thyme
1 teaspoon cayenne
1 teaspoon ground celery seeds
1 teaspoon salt
3 tablespoons grated onion or 1 teaspoon onion powder
2 garlic cloves, minced or 1 teaspoon garlic powder*

In a small bowl, stir together the paprika, white pepper, oregano, thyme, cayenne, celery seeds, and salt. If using the rub immediately, stir in the grated onion and minced garlic. If you are planning to store the rub in a tightly covered container for up to a month, add the onion and garlic powders. or add the fresh onion and garlic just before using the rub.

Rub onto the surface of the scallops or poultry, then let stand for 15 minutes at room temperature or refrigerate poultry up to 1 hour and scallops up to 30 minutes before grilling.

DOWNTOWN CAJUN RUB

Makes about ¼ cup; enough to rub on
1 (8- to 10-pound) turkey, 3 pounds of large or
jumbo peeled and deveined shrimp, 3 pounds of
salmon steaks, 3 pounds of beef burgers, or
3 pounds of chicken thighs or drumsticks

The heat comes from all directions in this rub, so use it on foods that can take it—such as sturdy seafood and dark meat of poultry. This is a close approximation of the blackened coating made famous several years ago in New Orleans, which remains popular today.

2 tablespoons chili powder
1 tablespoon paprika
1 teaspoon salt
1 teaspoon sugar
¾ teaspoon ground cumin
½ teaspoon coarsely ground black pepper
½ teaspoon cayenne
2 tablespoons grated onion or 1 teaspoon onion powder

In a small bowl, stir together the chili powder, paprika, salt, sugar, cumin, black pepper, and cayenne. If you are planning to store the rub in a tightly covered container for up to 1 month, add the onion powder, or add the grated onion just before grilling.

Rub onto the surface of the poultry, seafood, or burgers, then let stand for 15 minutes at room temperature, or refrigerate up to 1 hour before grilling.

JAMAICAN DRY RUB

Makes about 2 tablespoons; enough to rub on
2 ½ pounds of chicken parts or pork chops or
2 pounds of large or jumbo peeled and deveined shrimp

Jerk cooking is a specialty of the Caribbean, and Jamaica in particular. Though the herbs and spices are fairly constant, with allspice and peppers appearing in nearly every version, the combination can be applied as a dry rub, a wet paste, or in a marinade.

1½ teaspoons ground allspice
1 teaspoon dried thyme
1 teaspoon curry powder
1 teaspoon paprika
1 teaspoon sugar
½ teaspoon salt
½ teaspoon coarsely ground black pepper
½ teaspoon cayenne
¼ teaspoon grated nutmeg
¼ teaspoon ground cinnamon
⅛ teaspoon ground cloves

In a small bowl, stir together all ingredients. Use immediately or store in a tightly covered container for up to 1 month.

Rub onto the surface of the chicken, pork, or shrimp and let stand for 15 minutes at room temperature, or refrigerate chicken or pork up to 2 hours and shrimp up to 30 minutes before grilling.

GARAM MASALA

ί ί ί ί ί ί ί ί ί

Makes about 2 tablespoons; enough to rub on
2 pounds of chicken parts, lamb chops, swordfish steaks,
or jumbo peeled and deveined shrimp

Garam masala is a spice mix used in many Indian dishes, and the
particular combination depends on the preference of the cook.
This is a simple version, but does stay true to the tradition of
beginning with whole spices, toasting them lightly, and then grinding them. For the absolute best flavor, make the garam masala
shortly before you use it. It will keep well, but nothing matches
freshly toasted and ground spices.

3 tablespoons whole cardamom pods
½ cinnamon stick, broken into pieces
1 teaspoon whole black peppercorns
1 teaspoon whole coriander seeds
1 teaspoon whole cloves
1 teaspoon fenugreek seeds
½ teaspoon whole anise seeds
2 teaspoons ground turmeric

Break open the cardamom pods and scrape out the seeds,
which should measure about ¾ teaspoon. In a small skillet set over
medium heat, toss together the cardamom seeds, cinnamon stick,
peppercorns, coriander seeds, cloves, fenugreek seeds, and anise
seeds just until they become fragrant and turn a shade darker,
about 2 minutes. Immediately remove from the skillet and let cool

completely. Grind the spices using a mortar and pestle or an electric spice grinder. Stir in the turmeric. Use the spice mix within a day for best flavor.

Rub onto the chicken, lamb, or seafood and let stand 15 minutes at room temperature, or refrigerate up to 1 hour before grilling.

MOROCCAN RUB

ı ı ı ı ı ı ı ı ı

*Makes about 2 ½ tablespoons; enough to rub on
2 pounds of beef or lamb burgers, 2 pounds of beef or
lamb for shish kebab, or 2 ½ pounds of chicken parts*

This mild but complex mix of spices lends a mysteriously haunting flavor to even the most mundane of foods—rub it on ordinary beef burgers, then serve them in split pita breads garnished with chopped tomato and cucumber, and see what a difference a pinch of this and a pinch of that can make.

2 tablespoons paprika
1 teaspoon salt
1 teaspoon sugar
½ teaspoon coarsely ground black pepper
½ teaspoon ground ginger
½ teaspoon ground cardamom
½ teaspoon ground cumin
½ teaspoon ground fenugreek
¼ teaspoon ground cloves
¼ teaspoon ground cinnamon
¼ teaspoon ground allspice
¼ teaspoon cayenne

(continued)

In a small bowl, stir together all of the ingredients. Use immediately or store in a tightly covered container for up to 1 month.

Rub onto the meat or poultry and let stand 15 minutes or refrigerate up to 4 hours before grilling.

TENNESSEE RIB RUB

*Makes about 4 ½ tablespoons; enough to rub
onto 8 pounds of pork ribs or chops or steaks*

This is as close as I've ever come to duplicating the rub sold at my favorite Memphis rib hangout. I also like to smear it on pork chops or pork steaks before barbecuing, then simmer the grilled pork in Simple Simmering Sauce (page 98) until it is falling-apart tender. The rub is moderately hot, which is just the way it ought to be. Don't be a snob about the garlic and onion powders—that's the way it ought to be, too.

2 tablespoons coarsely ground black pepper
2 tablespoons sweet paprika
1 tablespoon sugar
1½ teaspoons garlic powder
1 teaspoon salt
1 teaspoon chili powder
1 teaspoon onion powder
½ teaspoon dry mustard

In a small bowl, stir together all of the ingredients. Use immediately or store in a tightly covered container for up to 1 month.

Rub onto the pork and let stand at room temperature 30 minutes or refrigerate for 2 to 8 hours before grilling.

INDIA SPICE RUB

*Makes about 2 tablespoons; enough to rub on 2 pounds of
chicken breasts, 1½ pounds of swordfish or halibut steaks,
2 pounds of peach or apricot halves, or 1 large pineapple, sliced*

This is a simplified spice mixture that gives an Indian flare to a
wide array of foods from fish to fowl. But for something really different,
sprinkle it on fresh pineapple slices or apricot or peach
halves, then grill just until softened. Drizzle the fruit with a little
honey and serve as an easy, but definitely exotic dessert.

2 teaspoons sugar
1 teaspoon ground cinnamon
1 teaspoon ground coriander
1 teaspoon ground cumin
½ teaspoon salt
½ teaspoon freshly ground black pepper
⅛ teaspoon cayenne

In a small bowl, stir together all of the ingredients. Use immediately,
or store in a tightly covered container for up to 1 month.

Rub onto the chicken or fish and let stand 15 minutes at room
temperature or refrigerate up to 1 hour before grilling. If rubbing
onto fruit, brush first with a light coating of vegetable oil or
melted butter, then grill over medium-low coals just until the fruit
begins to soften, about 5 minutes.

LEMON GARLIC AND FENNEL WET RUB

*Makes about 3 tablespoons; enough to rub on 1 pound
of tuna or swordfish steaks or boneless chicken breasts,
with or without skin, or 2 Cornish game hens*

Fennel and fish are a natural combination, but this mild rub is also excellent on chicken breasts. Grinding the fennel and pepper together is the secret.

1 tablespoon fennel seeds
1 teaspoon whole black peppercorns
½ teaspoon whole green peppercorns
2 large garlic cloves, minced
1 tablespoon grated lemon zest
2 teaspoons olive oil

Using a mortar and pestle or a spice grinder, grind together the fennel and peppercorns. Stir in the garlic, lemon zest, and olive oil.

Rub onto the surface of the fish or skinless chicken breasts. If using skin-on chicken breasts, use your fingers to loosen the skin, then rub the mixture underneath the skin onto the chicken. Let the fish or poultry stand at room temperature for 15 minutes or refrigerate up to 30 minutes before grilling.

CRACKED PEPPER QUINTUPLET

ι ι ι ι ι ι ι ι ι

*Makes about 3 tablespoons; enough to rub
on 2 pounds of beefsteak or beef burgers*

Every pepper has its own heat level and its own personality. Here's a quintet that will send skyrockets onto your tongue, but the little bit of honey will help to bring you back for more.

*1 tablespoon cracked black peppercorns
1 teaspoon ground white pepper
¼ teaspoon cayenne
1 jalapeño pepper, seeded and minced
1 tablespoon honey
1 teaspoon liquid hot pepper sauce*

In a small bowl, stir together the black and white peppers, cayenne, and jalapeño. Stir in the honey and hot pepper sauce until blended.

Rub onto the beef and let stand 15 minutes at room temperature or refrigerate up to 2 hours before grilling.

WALNUT AND BASIL PASTE

{ { { { { { { { {

*Makes about ¾ cup; enough to coat 2 pounds of boneless,
skinless chicken breasts or thighs or duck breasts or
2 pounds of tuna, swordfish, or salmon steaks or vegetables*

The ground walnuts toast as they coat and flavor the food during grilling. This rich paste protects and lends a pungent flavor to lean skinless poultry, fish steaks, and vegetables.

*1 cup lightly packed fresh basil leaves
3 garlic cloves, peeled
¾ cup walnut pieces
¼ cup grated Parmesan cheese
2 teaspoons red wine vinegar
1 tablespoon olive oil*

Place the basil in the work bowl of a food processor. With the motor running, drop in the garlic and process until basil and garlic are finely chopped, about 15 seconds. Add the walnuts, cheese, vinegar, and oil. Process to make a rough paste, about 20 seconds.

Smear evenly onto the poultry or fish or vegetables just before grilling.

SPICED TAHINI PASTE

*Makes about ¾ cup; enough to coat 1½ pounds of
skinless, boneless chicken breasts, 1½ pounds of large or
jumbo peeled and deveined shrimp, or 1½ pounds of
salmon or grouper fillets*

Yogurt forms a protective coating on foods, and the milk solids
caramelize during grilling to make a golden, richly flavored crust.
This mildly seasoned paste is especially good with thin cuts of
seafood or poultry.

6 tablespoons low-fat plain yogurt
½ cup tahini
2 tablespoons lemon juice
2 tablespoons chopped fresh mint
2 garlic cloves, minced
2 teaspoons ground cumin
1 teaspoon ground coriander

In a small bowl, gently whisk together the yogurt, tahini, and
lemon juice until blended. Stir in the mint, garlic, cumin, and
coriander. Refrigerate the paste, covered, for at least 1 hour and up
to 6 hours before using. Smear onto the poultry or seafood just
before grilling.

ADOBADO PASTE

ʔ ʔ ʔ ʔ ʔ ʔ ʔ ʔ ʔ

Makes about ⅓ cup; enough to coat 1 pound of redfish or grouper fillets, 1 pound of large or jumbo peeled and deveined shrimp, 2 pounds of chicken parts, or 1 pound of vegetables

The heat here depends upon the brand and strength of the chili powder that you use. In any case, however, the molasses softens the blow a bit, and gives this paste an interesting sweet/hot quality.

¼ cup chili powder
3 tablespoons lime juice
1½ tablespoons molasses
1 teaspoon red wine vinegar
2 large garlic cloves, minced

In a small bowl, stir together all of the ingredients until blended. Let stand at least 15 minutes or up to 1 hour at room temperature before using. Smear onto the seafood or poultry and let stand 15 minutes at room temperature or refrigerate poultry up to 2 hours before grilling.

CHOOSE-YOUR-HEAT
JERK PASTE

ι ι ι ι ι ι ι ι ι

*Makes about ½ cup; enough to coat 2 pounds
of chicken parts or pork chops or 4 pounds of pork spareribs*

Though very tiny, serrano peppers pack a huge wallop. Only
slightly less fiery on the heat scale are jalapeños. You can control
the potency by varying the amount of either one. So choose according to your company and how much you want to heat them up.

*¼ cup finely chopped scallions
1 to 2 tablespoons minced serrano or jalapeño peppers
1 garlic clove, minced
1 tablespoon ground allspice
1 teaspoon ground cinnamon
½ teaspoon ground mace
½ teaspoon salt
1 tablespoon olive oil
2 teaspoons red wine vinegar*

In a small bowl, stir together the scallions, peppers, garlic, allspice, cinnamon, mace, and salt. Stir in the oil and vinegar. Let the
paste stand for at least 15 minutes or up to 2 hours before using.
Smear onto the chicken or pork and let stand 15 minutes at room
temperature or refrigerate up to 2 hours before grilling.

SAMBAL PASTE

ι ι ι ι ι ι ι ι ι

*Makes about ¾ cup; enough to coat 3 pounds of
chicken parts or lamb chops or 2 pounds of
ground beef or lamb patties*

Every culture worth its "salt and pepper" has its classic hot sauces
and condiments. Indian cuisine is among the more advanced in the
subtle nuances of using hot peppers. Here they are enhanced with
herbs, enriched with a nut paste, and tempered by a touch of
honey. The result is a slow burn with a lovely taste afterglow.

½ cup lightly packed cilantro sprigs
½ cup lightly packed fresh mint leaves
¼ cup unsalted cashews
1 or 2 jalapeño peppers, seeded and minced
1 tablespoon honey
1 tablespoon sherry vinegar
1 teaspoon peanut oil

Place the cilantro, mint, cashews, and jalapeño(s) in the work
bowl of a food processor. Process to make a rough paste, about 30
seconds, stopping once or twice to scrape down the work bowl.
Add the honey, vinegar, and oil. Process until well blended, about
10 seconds. Let stand 15 minutes or up to 2 hours at room temperature before using.

Smear onto the chicken or meat and let stand 15 minutes at
room temperature or up to 1 hour in the refrigerator before grilling.

ANNATTO RUM PASTE

~ ~ ~ ~ ~ ~ ~ ~ ~

Makes about ¾ cup; enough to coat 3 pounds of
chicken parts or pork chops or 2 pounds of boneless
beefsteak or pork tenderloin

Annatto, which is also called achiote, is a common ingredient in
Mexican and Caribbean marinades and sauces. It is sold as seeds,
which must be heated in order to release the rich, mellow peppery
flavor. It is also sold as a paste, which I prefer because it is easier
to combine with other ingredients. For either type, look in Latin
markets and large supermarkets for jars of seeds or paste with a
brick-red color. A darker hue means that the product has been sit-
ting on the shelf too long and has probably lost potency.

½ cup (4 ounces) achiote paste
2 tablespoons lime juice
2 tablespoons dark rum
2 teaspoons vegetable oil
½ teaspoon ground cumin
½ teaspoon freshly ground black pepper
½ teaspoon salt
¼ teaspoon ground cinnamon
2 garlic cloves, minced

In a food processor, puree the achiote paste, lime juice, rum,
and oil, about 10 seconds. Add the cumin, pepper, salt, cinnamon,
and garlic, and process just to blend, about 5 seconds. Let stand for
at least 1 hour or up to 4 hours at room temperature before using.

Smear onto chicken or meat and let stand 15 minutes at room
temperature or refrigerate up to 2 hours before grilling.

GREEN CURRY PASTE

*Makes about ¾ cup; enough to coat 2 pounds of skinless,
boneless chicken breasts, 2 pounds of pork tenderloin,
3 pounds of lamb chops, or 2 pounds of swordfish steaks*

Curry pastes of several flavors are now widely available in the
Asian sections of large supermarkets. They are the basis of many
excellent sauces, but take on a whole new dimension when
exposed to the smoky heat of a grill. Green curry is milder than
red curry, and has a lovely, complex flavor.

⅓ cup unsweetened canned coconut milk
⅓ cup Thai green curry paste
2 teaspoons vegetable oil
2 tablespoons finely chopped lemongrass or
   2 teaspoons grated lemon zest

In a small bowl, stir all of the ingredients together. Let stand at
least 15 minutes or up to 2 hours at room temperature before using.
   Smear onto chicken or meat and let stand 15 minutes at room
temperature or refrigerate up to 2 hours before grilling. Smear
onto fish just before grilling.

ROASTED GARLIC PASTE

꿈 꿈 꿈 꿈 꿈 꿈 꿈 꿈 꿈

*Makes about ¼ cup; enough to coat 1½ pounds of
skinless, boneless chicken breasts, pork or veal cutlets,
tuna steaks, or vegetables*

Roasted garlic spreads like butter and nicely lends its dusky, mellow flavor to grilling pastes. Here it is the headline ingredient, showcased best when smeared onto thin, quick-cooking cuts of meat or poultry. Choose large, firm, unblemished heads of garlic for roasting.

2 large heads of garlic, separated into cloves and peeled
2 tablespoons olive oil, preferably extra-virgin
1 tablespoon balsamic vinegar
½ teaspoon salt
¼ teaspoon dried hot pepper flakes

Preheat the oven to 350 degrees. Place the garlic cloves on a sheet of heavy-duty aluminum foil. Drizzle with 1 tablespoon of the oil. Wrap tightly in the foil and roast until the cloves are very soft, about 30 minutes. Let cool, then mash with the remaining oil, using the back of a spoon to make a fairly smooth paste. Stir in the vinegar, salt, and pepper flakes. Use immediately or let stand up to 2 hours before using.

Smear onto the chicken, meat, or fish just before grilling.

CEYLON TEA PASTE

Makes about ⅔ cup; enough to coat 3 pounds of
chicken parts, 2 split duck breasts, 2 (1½-pound) lobsters,
or 2 pounds of large or jumbo peeled and deveined shrimp

Personalize this mild paste by using your favorite tea leaf blend.
The leaves roast to a rich full flavor during grilling. Although versatile, it is really wonderful on lobster or lobster tails.

⅓ cup loose tea leaves
5 whole cloves
3 star anise or ¾ teaspoon anise seeds
1½ tablespoons grated orange zest
¼ cup thawed frozen orange juice concentrate
¼ teaspoon ground cinnamon

In a spice grinder or using a mortar and pestle, grind together
the tea leaves, cloves, star anise or anise seeds, and orange zest.
Place in a small bowl, then stir in the orange juice concentrate and
cinnamon to blend. Let stand 15 minutes or refrigerate up to 2
hours before using.

Smear onto the chicken, duck, or seafood, and let stand 15
minutes at room temperature or refrigerate poultry and seafood up
to 1 hour before grilling.

PEPPERY LEMONADE PASTE

~ ~ ~ ~ ~ ~ ~ ~ ~

Makes about ½ cup; enough to coat 1½ pounds
of boneless pork or veal cutlets

This sweet/hot paste caramelizes quickly so it should be used on thin cuts that cook very fast.

¼ cup thawed frozen lemonade concentrate
1 tablespoon olive oil
2 teaspoons red wine vinegar
3 garlic cloves, minced
½ teaspoon dried hot pepper flakes

In a small bowl, stir together all of the ingredients. Let stand at least 15 minutes at room temperature or refrigerate up to 2 hours before using.

Coat the meat just before grilling.

WASABI SCALLION PASTE

~ ~ ~ ~ ~ ~ ~ ~ ~ ~

*Makes about ⅓ cup; enough to coat 1½ pounds
of swordfish or tuna steaks or 1 pound of large or
jumbo peeled and deveined shrimp*

Wasabi is Japanese horseradish, commonly available as a powder
that when reconstituted in water becomes a searingly hot condiment. It is a classic sushi ingredient, but is also terrific as the basis
for a seafood grilling paste.

2 teaspoons wasabi powder
½ teaspoon dry mustard
3 star anise or ½ teaspoon anise seeds
2 tablespoons mirin or dry sherry
2 tablespoons reduced-sodium soy sauce
1 tablespoon vegetable oil

In a small bowl, dissolve the wasabi and dry mustard in 1
tablespoon of cold water. In a mortar and pestle or in a spice
grinder, crush the star anise or anise seeds. Add the crushed anise
to the wasabi paste along with the mirin, soy sauce, and oil. Let
stand at least 15 minutes or up to 2 hours at room temperature
before using.

Coat the seafood just before grilling.

ASIAN SESAME
PEANUT PASTE

≀ ≀ ≀ ≀ ≀ ≀ ≀ ≀ ≀

*Makes about ½ cup; enough to coat 2 pounds of beefsteak,
pork tenderloin, boneless, skinless chicken breasts or thighs,
or 2 split duck breasts*

This is one of my favorite pastes for beefsteak, but pork tenderloins and chicken also take nicely to the moderately hot coating.
The sliced meat or chicken is especially good served as a salad over
greens and slivered red peppers dressed with a soy and rice wine
vinaigrette.

*¼ cup sesame seeds
2 tablespoons hoisin sauce
1 tablespoon smooth peanut butter
2 teaspoons grated fresh ginger
¼ teaspoon dried hot pepper flakes*

Lightly toast the sesame seeds by tossing in a small dry skillet
set over medium heat just until fragrant and a shade darker in
color, about 2 minutes. Immediately remove the seeds from the
pan and let cool completely. In a small bowl, blend together the
seeds, hoisin sauce, peanut butter, ginger, and pepper flakes. Use
immediately or let stand up to 4 hours at room temperature before
using.

Coat meat or poultry just before grilling.

BETTER THAN
BUFFALO PASTE

*Makes about ½ cup; enough to coat 3 pounds
of chicken wings or cut-up chicken parts*

Buffalo, New York, may have made chicken wings one of
America's most popular bar nibbles, but a good idea can usually
be expanded upon. Achiote seeds and dried ground ancho chiles,
both available in Latin markets, make an eye-watering hot paste.
To give these wings a Southwest presentation, substitute jicama
sticks for the usual celery, and stir a little lime juice into the traditional blue cheese dressing.

2 dried ancho chiles
2 tablespoons achiote seeds
1 tablespoon honey
1 tablespoon vegetable oil
1 teaspoon whole black peppercorns
1 teaspoon grated orange zest
½ teaspoon ground allspice
½ teaspoon salt

Scrape out and discard the seeds from the chiles, and break the
chiles into pieces. Place the chiles and achiote seeds in a food
processor along with the remaining ingredients. Process to make a
rough puree, about 30 seconds, scraping down the sides of the
work bowl once or twice. Let the paste stand for at least 15 minutes or up to 6 hours at room temperature before using.

Coat the chicken and let stand 15 minutes at room temperature or refrigerate up to 1 hour before grilling.

PROVENÇAL ROSEMARY AND CITRUS PASTE

*Makes about ⅓ cup; enough to coat 1½ pounds
of boneless, skinless chicken breasts or veal
cutlets; 1½ pounds of swordfish steaks or large or jumbo
peeled and deveined shrimp or large sea scallops;
or 2 ½ pounds of veal chops*

This is a delightful summery paste for all sorts of delicate foods. When zesting the fruit, use a small sharp knife or a zester, and be careful to cut only deep enough to get the colored part. The white pith is bitter, so leave it behind.

*2 tablespoons chopped fresh rosemary
1 tablespoon grated lemon zest
1 tablespoon grated orange zest
1 tablespoon grated grapefruit zest
2 garlic cloves, minced
½ teaspoon salt
1 jalapeño pepper, minced
1 tablespoon olive oil
2 teaspoons lemon juice*

In a small bowl, stir together the rosemary, all citrus zests, garlic, salt, and jalapeño pepper. Stir in the olive oil and lemon juice. Let stand at least 15 minutes or up to 1 hour at room temperature before using.

Coat the chicken, meat, or seafood and let stand 15 minutes at room temperature, or refrigerate meat or poultry for up to 1 hour before grilling. Seafood should be grilled right away.

BRITISH BARBECUE PASTE

*Makes about ½ cup; enough to coat 3 pounds
of lamb chops or 2 pounds of beefsteak*

We may not associate the British Isles with great barbecue, but these folks do know more than a thing or two about grilling meats, especially lamb or beef. And no one grows herbs better than the British. Hence the following savory paste.

*¼ cup grated onion
2 tablespoons chopped fresh thyme
1 tablespoon vegetable oil
1 teaspoon sherry vinegar
1 teaspoon dry mustard powder
1 teaspoon ground celery seeds*

In a small bowl, stir together all of the ingredients. Let stand for 15 minutes at room temperature or refrigerate up to 2 hours before using.

Coat the meat and let stand 15 minutes before grilling.

TANGERINE CHIPOTLE PASTE

ι ι ι ι ι ι ι ι ι

*Makes about ⅓ cup; enough to coat 2 ½ pounds
of pork chops or chicken parts or 4 pounds
of pork spareribs*

Chipotles in adobo are smoked jalapeños canned in a spicy tomato and onion sauce. They are a wonderful ingredient to keep on hand and are increasingly available wherever Latin foods are stocked in the supermarket. This simple paste is an example of their versatility.

*3 tablespoons thawed frozen tangerine or orange juice concentrate
3 canned chipotles, finely chopped
1½ tablespoons adobo sauce from the canned chipotles*

In a small bowl, stir to combine all of the ingredients. Use immediately or refrigerate up to 6 hours before using.

Coat the meat or chicken and let stand 15 minutes at room temperature or refrigerate up to 2 hours before grilling.

BROWN SUGAR CURE

*Makes about ½ cup; enough to coat 2 pounds of
ham steaks or salmon fillets or steaks, 2 ½ pounds of
pork chops, or 4 pounds of spareribs*

This is the perfect paste or glaze for ham steaks, but it is also wonderful on salmon fillets or steaks.

3 tablespoons prepared Chinese mustard or spicy brown mustard
3 tablespoons brown sugar
2 tablespoons reduced-sodium soy sauce
2 teaspoons rice wine vinegar
1 teaspoon coarsely ground black pepper

In a small bowl, stir together all of the ingredients. Let stand at least 15 minutes or up to 3 hours at room temperature before using.

Coat the ham steaks or fish just before grilling. Coat the pork chops or ribs during the last 10 minutes of grilling time.

Condiments

∼ ∼ ∼ ∼ ∼ ∼ ∼ ∼ ∼

Condiments

The word "condiment" comes from the Latin *condimentum*, which loosely translates to pickle or seasoning. Condiments are considered to be seasonings that are added at the table rather than in the kitchen. But if you are like me, the best definition of a condiment is anything that is on the shelf of the refrigerator door.

Ketchup, mustard, pickles, and relish seem to be among the staple foods in nearly every household in America. Because we use them so often, we take them for granted. Furthermore, most people tend to think that condiments are something made by big companies or small boutique shops, but certainly never at home.

Because of that, we often limit our condiment selection to the choices given to us by the local grocer.

There is a world of condiments beyond tomato ketchup and yellow mustard, pickle relish and standard mayonnaise. And many of them are easy to make—some from scratch and some built on a commercial product base.

Condiments turn a very good barbecue into something quite memorable. Every major cuisine has its own heritage of condiments—mustard, for example, is found in cuisines ranging from Chinese to Scandinavian, and German to French. In each country, mustard is interpreted quite differently, and is integral to the character of the cuisine itself. In America, we have practically defined our condiment cupboard by tomato ketchup, but in the world of ketchups, very few have tomatoes at all.

Since condiments are common and traditional accompaniments to grilled foods and integral to their enjoyment (who ever had a hot dog without mustard?), it is well worth taking a look at personalizing your condiment shelf with a few homemade variations on the theme.

Like barbecue sauces and dry rubs, most condiments keep well in the refrigerator and make terrific gifts.

PLUM KETCHUP

₹ ₹ ₹ ₹ ₹ ₹ ₹ ₹ ₹

Makes about 3 cups; use for burgers, steaks, pork, and chicken

Any ripe plum can be used here, but deep red or purple varieties give a particularly rich color to this very spicy ketchup. The Asian chile sauce already has garlic and peppers in it, so you can personalize the heat of your ketchup by adjusting the amount of the chile sauce, which is found in most well-stocked supermarkets.

1 pound fresh plums, preferably red or purple plums
1 medium onion, chopped
¼ cup orange juice
3 tablespoons dark brown sugar
3 tablespoons rice wine vinegar
3 tablespoons Asian hot chile sauce with garlic
1 tablespoon reduced-sodium soy sauce
1 tablespoon grated fresh ginger
1 teaspoon dry mustard
½ teaspoon salt

Place all ingredients in a nonreactive saucepan and bring just to a boil, stirring to dissolve the sugar. Reduce the heat to medium and simmer, uncovered and stirring often, until the sauce is thickened and the liquid is reduced by nearly half, 30 to 40 minutes. Remove from the heat and let cool. (The sauce will thicken further as it cools.)

The ketchup can be stored, covered, in the refrigerator for up to 1 month. Serve at room temperature.

ANCHO CHILE AND MANGO KETCHUP

ί ί ί ί ί ί ί ί ί

Makes about 1½ cups; use for fish steaks,
pork tenderloin, or chicken

The heady perfume of a ripe mango meets its match in the deep
dusky flavor of ancho chiles. Together they produce a ketchup that
at first tingles the tongue with sweetness, and then the slow after-
burn of chile heat begins to take over—sort of like giving your
mouth a day on a tropical beach.

2 dried ancho chiles
2 large ripe mangoes
¼ cup lemon juice
2 tablespoons orange juice
2 tablespoons honey
1 tablespoon grated fresh ginger
½ teaspoon salt
¼ teaspoon dried hot pepper flakes
6 whole allspice
6 whole cloves
1 cinnamon stick, broken in half

Place the chiles in a small deep bowl and cover them with boiling water. Let the chiles stand until softened, 20 to 30 minutes.
Peel the mangoes and cut the fruit into chunks.

Drain the softened chiles and remove the stems and seeds. Tear
the chiles into small pieces and puree them in a food processor.
Add the mangoes to the work bowl and process to a coarse puree.

Transfer the mangoes and chiles to a medium saucepan. Stir in the lemon and orange juices, honey, ginger, salt, and pepper flakes. Tie the allspice, cloves, and cinnamon stick in a small mesh or cheesecloth bag and add to the saucepan.

Bring the mixture to a simmer over medium heat. Reduce the heat to low and simmer gently, uncovered and stirring often, until thickened, about 15 minutes. Let cool.

The ketchup can be stored, covered, in the refrigerator for up to 1 month. Serve at room temperature.

CRANBERRY KETCHUP

ʒ ʒ ʒ ʒ ʒ ʒ ʒ ʒ ʒ ʒ

Makes about 1½ cups; use for burgers, chicken, turkey, duck, pork chops or tenderloin, or ham

Fresh or frozen cranberries can be used in this recipe, but if you can't find either one, try the variation for dried cranberries. These are usually sweeter, and no extra sugar is needed. Either version makes a wonderfully tangy, brilliant red, non-tomato "ketchup."

2 cups fresh or frozen cranberries (see Note)
½ cup chopped onion
½ cup sugar
½ cup fresh orange juice
2 tablespoons red wine vinegar
2 tablespoons grated fresh or prepared horseradish
Salt and pepper

In a medium saucepan, combine the cranberries, onion, sugar, and orange juice. Bring to a boil, stirring to dissolve the sugar. Then reduce the heat to medium-low and simmer, stirring often, until the cranberries are soft and most have popped, about 8 minutes. Stir in the vinegar and horseradish, and simmer for 2 minutes. Season to taste with salt and pepper and let cool.

The ketchup can be stored, covered, in the refrigerator up to 1 month. Serve slightly warm or at room temperature.

Note: If you wish to use dried cranberries, omit the sugar and increase the orange juice to ¾ cup. In a small saucepan, bring the cranberries, onion, and orange juice to a simmer over medium heat, stirring often, until the cranberries are plumped and softened, about 5 minutes. If the cranberries seem dry, add a few more tablespoons of orange juice. Add the vinegar, horseradish, salt, and pepper as directed above.

CIRCUS DOG MUSTARD

Makes about 2 cups; use for hot dogs and hamburgers

We went to the circus every summer when I was a child. My fondest food memory is hot dogs on a bun slathered with golden pan-fried onions and peppers simmered in mustard. Summer and the circus are still magical times for me, so I have made this mustard for my children since they were little. They call it Circus Dog Mustard.

3 tablespoons vegetable oil
1 large onion, coarsely chopped
1 large green pepper, coarsely chopped
2 garlic cloves, minced
½ teaspoon celery seeds
¼ cup Dijon mustard

In a large skillet, heat the oil and cook the onion and green pepper over medium-low heat, stirring often, until the vegetables are softened and tinged with gold, about 10 minutes. Add the garlic and celery seeds. Continue to cook for 5 minutes. Stir in the mustard and cook, stirring, for 3 minutes to blend flavors.

The mustard sauce can be used immediately or cooled and refrigerated, covered, for up to 2 days. Reheat gently to use.

CILANTRO MUSTARD MAYONNAISE

ર ર ર ર ર ર ર ર ર

*Makes about 1 cup; use for hot dogs,
hamburgers, pork chops, and spareribs, fish steaks
such as salmon or swordfish, or shrimp*

This easy mustard sauce goes together in seconds. In addition to elevating burgers and hot dogs to a new level, it also makes a good dip for raw vegetables.

*½ cup Dijon mustard
½ cup mayonnaise, regular or reduced-fat
⅓ cup chopped cilantro
1 tablespoon chili powder
1 teaspoon ground cumin*

In a small bowl, stir together all of the ingredients. Cover and refrigerate for at least 1 hour or up to 3 days before using.

MAPLE MUSTARD SAUCE

ز ز ز ز ز ز ز ز ز

Makes about ¾ cup; use for ham steak, winter squash, or fruit

Because of its rich maple sweetness, this is wonderful on grilled winter squash slices. But it is a real star as a dessert sauce spooned over grilled fruits, especially peaches.

½ cup pure maple syrup
½ cup smooth Dijon mustard

In a small saucepan, simmer the maple syrup until reduced to about ¼ cup, about 10 minutes. Raise the heat to low and stir in the mustard. Simmer gently, stirring until the sauce is smooth and thick, about 5 minutes.

Serve the sauce slightly warm. Store, covered, in the refrigerator, for up to 3 days. Reheat gently to serve.

MEDITERRANEAN OLIVE SPREAD

ک ک ک ک ک ک ک ک ک

*Makes about ⅔ cup; use for fish steaks such as tuna
and swordfish, peeled and deveined shrimp, boneless
chicken, or grilled bread*

This is a potent condiment that packs a lot of flavor when spread thinly. It is especially delicious on grilled bread, which is then topped with diced summer tomatoes to make an instant bruschetta. Use the best-quality olives you can find.

½ cup black or green Mediterranean olives, pitted
¼ cup sun-dried tomatoes packed in oil
1 large garlic clove, minced
3 tablespoons lemon juice
2 tablespoons bottled ketchup
¼ cup chopped fresh basil
¼ teaspoon dried hot pepper flakes

In a food processor, coarsely puree the olives, tomatoes, and garlic. Add the lemon juice, ketchup, basil, and pepper flakes. Pulse to blend. Let the olive spread stand at room temperature for at least 30 minutes or refrigerate up to 4 days before using. Serve at room temperature.

ROASTED GARLIC GUACAMOLE

ʔ ʔ ʔ ʔ ʔ ʔ ʔ ʔ ʔ

*Makes about 2 cups; use for beefsteak such
as skirt steaks, pork tenderloin or chops, fish steaks
such as swordfish, or peeled and deveined shrimp*

Roasted garlic brings a new character to the avocado in this variation on the classic guacamole. It's great for fajitas, but also just as
good as a dip for vegetables, tortilla chips, or salsa.

4 large garlic cloves, peeled
2 teaspoons olive oil
1 large ripe avocado
1½ tablespoons lime juice
1 jalapeño pepper, seeded and finely minced
Salt and white pepper

Preheat the oven to 350 degrees or prepare a barbecue fire if
you plan to grill other foods. Place the garlic in the center of a
small piece of heavy-duty or double-thickness aluminum foil.
Drizzle with the olive oil, then wrap the garlic in the foil. Roast or
grill until the garlic is softened, about 30 minutes. Let the garlic
cool.

Peel and pit the avocado, and cut the fruit into chunks. In a
food processor, coarsely puree the avocado with the garlic, lime
juice, and jalapeño. Season to taste with salt and pepper. Chill the
guacamole, covered, for at least 15 minutes or up to 4 hours
before serving.

KUTZTOWN PICKLE RELISH

ᘛ ᘛ ᘛ ᘛ ᘛ ᘛ ᘛ ᘛ ᘛ

Makes about 3 cups; use for burgers, steaks,
hot dogs, ham steaks, or pork chops

Don't discard that watermelon rind! Thrifty Pennsylvania Dutch cooks have long known that it makes a great pickle relish. And if you have a really big watermelon, make this recipe in quantities. It keeps in the refrigerator for several weeks and makes a terrific gift in case you are invited to someone else's house for a barbecue!

Rind from ¼ large watermelon
2 tablespoons salt
1 cup cider vinegar
⅔ cup sugar
4 whole allspice
4 whole cloves
4 black peppercorns
1 cinnamon stick, broken in half
2 thin slices fresh ginger
2 2-inch strips lemon peel, colored part only

Cut off all of the pink fruit from the watermelon rind and discard. Cut the rind into 1-inch cubes and place in a medium bowl. Dissolve the salt in 3 cups of water and pour over the watermelon. Push the rind down to submerge in the brine. If the brine doesn't completely cover, add a small amount of water as needed. Cover the bowl and let the rind stand 6 hours at room temperature or overnight in the refrigerator.

(continued)

Drain the rind and rinse thoroughly under cold water. Place the rind in a saucepan and cover with fresh water. Simmer gently over medium-low heat until just fork-tender, about 18 minutes.

Meanwhile, in a large saucepan, bring the vinegar, sugar, and ⅓ cup of water to a boil, stirring to dissolve the sugar. Add the allspice, cloves, peppercorns, cinnamon, ginger, lemon peel, and the watermelon cubes.

Partially cover the pan and simmer over medium-low heat until the watermelon is tender and translucent, about 20 minutes. Let the pickles cool in the syrup, then chill at least 12 hours or up to 4 weeks before using. (If a milder pickle is desired, remove the spices from the syrup after 12 hours.)

CHILE LIME BUTTER

*Makes ¼ cup; use for fish steaks such as salmon,
halibut, or swordfish, boneless chicken breasts,
or any grilled summer vegetable, especially corn on the cob*

Flavored butters are nice to have on hand to dress up plain grilled seafood, poultry, or vegetables. You can substitute orange or grapefruit for the lime zest, if you wish.

*4 tablespoons softened unsalted butter
1 tablespoon grated lime zest
½ teaspoon ground cumin
1 jalapeño, seeded and finely minced*

In a small dish, combine all of the ingredients. Let stand at least 15 minutes before using, or refrigerate in the dish or formed into a roll, then wrapped in plastic. The butter can be stored up to 3 days. Remove from the refrigerator at least 15 minutes before using.

LEMON YOGURT AIOLI

ƺ ƺ ƺ ƺ ƺ ƺ ƺ ƺ ƺ

Makes about 1 cup; use for all seafood or any grilled
vegetable, especially broccoli or asparagus

The lemon and yogurt add a light and contemporary twist to a
classic sauce.

¾ cup plain low-fat yogurt
½ cup mayonnaise, regular or reduced-fat
1 tablespoon lemon juice
2 teaspoons grated lemon zest
3 garlic cloves, minced
Salt and white pepper

Spoon the yogurt into a sieve or strainer lined with cheesecloth. Set the sieve over a mixing bowl. Let the yogurt drain for 30
to 45 minutes until it is reduced to about ½ cup.

In a small bowl, stir together the yogurt, mayonnaise, lemon
juice and zest, and the garlic. Season to taste with salt and white
pepper.

Chill the aioli for at least 1 hour or up to 6 hours before using.
Serve at cool room temperature.

GORGONZOLA
YOGURT SAUCE

Makes about ¾ cup; use for beefsteak, burgers, or lamb

This is my favorite topping for steak.

¾ cup plain low-fat yogurt
⅓ cup Gorgonzola cheese
3 tablespoons chopped chives
1 teaspoon Worcestershire sauce
½ teaspoon hot pepper sauce

Spoon the yogurt into a sieve or strainer lined with cheese-cloth. Set the sieve over a mixing bowl. Let the yogurt drain for 30 to 45 minutes until it is reduced to about ½ cup.

In a small bowl, mash the Gorgonzola with the back of a spoon. Stir in the yogurt, chives, Worcestershire, and hot pepper sauces.

Let the sauce stand for 15 to 30 minutes before using, or refrigerate up to 24 hours. Serve at cool room temperature.

CURRY AND
MINT RAITA

Makes about 2 cups; use for lamb, beef, or grilled vegetables

This is a simple version of the cooling sauce that is a classic part of Indian cooking. It also makes a fine dip for raw vegetables.

1½ cups plain low-fat yogurt
1 tablespoon curry powder
1 cup diced peeled cucumber
½ cup chopped red onion
3 tablespoons chopped fresh mint
Salt and cayenne pepper

Spoon the yogurt into a sieve or strainer lined with cheesecloth. Set the sieve over a mixing bowl. Let the yogurt drain for 30 to 45 minutes until it is reduced to about 1 cup.

Meanwhile, stir the curry powder in a small skillet set over medium heat just until it is fragrant, about 1 minute. Immediately scrape the curry powder into a mixing bowl. Stir in the thickened yogurt, cucumber, onion, and mint. Season to taste with salt and cayenne pepper.

Chill the raita for at least 30 minutes or up to 8 hours before using. Remove from the refrigerator 15 minutes before serving at cool room temperature.

Index

~ ~ ~ ~ ~ ~ ~ ~ ~